KNITTING *loves* CROCHET

KNITTING *loves* CROCHET

22 Stylish Designs to Hook Up Your Knitting with a Touch of Crochet

CANDI JENSEN

Photography by Donna Demari

Storey Publishing

The mission of Storey Publishing is to serve our customers
by publishing practical information that encourages personal independence
in harmony with the environment.

Edited by Gwen Steege and Candie Frankel

Art direction by Mary Velgos

Cover and text design by Mary Velgos

Text production by Jessica Armstrong

Photographs © by Donna Demari; decorative and technical details
    by Adam Mastoon

Photo styling by Robin Tesoro

Illustrations by Christine Erikson

Indexed by Susan Olason, Indexes & Knowledge Maps

The information in this book is true and complete to the best of our knowledge.
All recommendations are made without guarantee on the part of the author or Storey
Publishing. The author and publisher disclaim any liability in connection with the use
of this information. For additional information please contact Storey Publishing,
210 MASS MoCA Way, North Adams, MA 01247.

Storey books are available for special premium and promotional uses and for customized
editions. For further information, please call 1-800-793-9396.

Printed in Hong Kong by Elegance.

10 9 8 7 6 5 4 3 2 1

LIBRARY OF CONGRESS CATALOGING-IN-PUBLICATION DATA

Jensen, Candi.
    Knitting loves crochet : 22 stylish designs to hook up your knitting with a touch of crochet /
Candi Jensen ; photography by Donna Demari.
        p. cm.
    Includes index.
    ISBN-13: 978-1-58017-842-6; ISBN-10: 1-58017-842-1 (pbk. : alk. paper)
    1. Crocheting — Patterns. 2. Knitting — Patterns. I. Title.

TT825.J4824 2006
746.43'4041 — dc22
                                                                            2006015032

Dedicated to all the knitters and crocheters
who inspire me to keep the designs flowing, and
to the home crew — Tommy, Skeeter, Lilac, and
Calvin — who keep me laughing.

Contents

p. 5

p. 41

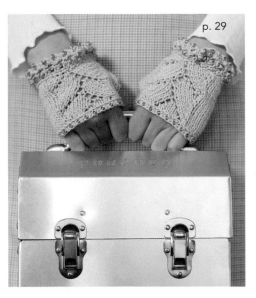

p. 29

p. 101

p. 135

CHAPTER 3 Touch of Home 142

p. 155

p. 145

p. 61

a love affair with Stitches

"KNITTING LOVES CROCHET" says it all! This book is a real labor of love, because it gives me a chance to share my enthusiasm for both knitting and crochet. Some of you know me only as a crochet designer; others know just the knitting designs I've created over the years. In truth, I've always worked with both, and I've always wanted to do a book that incorporates the strengths and best traits of each. ✑ With knitting, for instance, you can work ribbing with a good deal of stretch for a nice snug fit around waist and wrists, whereas crochet used for this purpose would be a bit inflexible and bulky. On the other hand, crochet creates a dense, even bulky fabric, depending on the yarn you use, resulting in a fabric that has a wonderful texture and that lies flat without any assistance from special stitches. It's easier to create drape with a knitted fabric, but the quality that makes the fabric drape can also cause it to curl along the edges. Because of the way the stitches are twisted, cables are a hallmark of knitting, but when you need a lacy edging, crochet is the way to go. As you can see, both knitting and crochet have their virtues, and when combined in a single garment, pillow, or throw, the match can create a dazzling effect. ∽ All too often, crochet has been perceived as the "dowdy" craft and knitting as the "elegant" one. Now that the fashion gurus have deemed crochet the current "in" look, crochet's cachet has risen, but sometimes I still feel that I have to be a cheerleader for crochet. It's time for dyed-in-the-wool knitters to turn over a new leaf and embrace crochet for the beautiful, versatile craft that it is. I'm hoping that the designs in this book demonstrate the many ways you can use knitting and crochet to show off the best qualities of both. ∽ If you're an experienced knitter and haven't tried crochet, it's time to pick up that hook and begin to experiment. If your main pastime is crochet, you can confidently pick up the sticks and enjoy working your favorite crochet stitches into knitted items. You'll find that most of the projects in this book are well within the capabilities of the average knitter, with a few challenges thrown in for fun. After all, life would be boring without challenges! Simply open your mind to the possibility that you can create with both techniques, and let's get started.

HOOK AND NEEDLE

It's sometimes said that crocheting is easier than knitting because it takes only one stick instead of two. But, of course, each tool has particular characteristics that make it possible to carry out the techniques required for its craft. (For a chart showing hook and needle sizes, see page 187.) Here's a little refresher course on the structure and vocabulary of each.

Getting Hooked

Although there are several different types of crochet hooks, they all have one thing in common: a hook at the end. You catch and manipulate the yarn with the *head* and *throat*, which are located at the end of your crochet hook. Behind the head is the *shank*, followed by a flat portion called the *grip*, and finally the *handle*. The grip is where you place your fingers to control the hook.

Straight versus circular, bamboo versus plastic — we all have our preference for what's nicest to use. I tend to like short bamboo needles because they're so light, although I do sometimes have to cram all the stitches into a short space. Some knitters prefer circular needles because they don't get in the way. The only way to discover what you prefer is to try out different kinds and see what works best for you.

Getting Loopy

Both knitting and crochet involve linking a series of loops, but each technique connects the loops in a different way. Although there are many variations in both knitting and crochet, here's a very basic description of what happens in each.

To work a knit stitch, you draw up a loop through the first stitch on the left-hand needle, place the loop on the right-hand needle, and let the original stitch drop, which locks it into the developing fabric.

To work a crochet stitch, you use the hook to draw one or more loops through an opening (a stitch or a ring, for instance). The stitch is complete when you insert the hook to begin a new stitch. If you pull two, three, or more loops through a stitch at a time, you can make a denser fabric than with knitting; this kind of

knit stitch

crochet stitch

Labels on crochet hook: handle, shank, throat, grip, head

crochet may use up to one-third more yarn. On the other hand, you can also work crochet stitches to create very open, lacelike effects.

ALL YARN IS NOT CREATED EQUAL

Although you can knit or crochet with many varieties of yarns, certain types may be more appropriate for one or the other technique. When you knit, all your stitches are in plain sight on the needles, making it easy to identify individual stitches, no matter how bumpy, lumpy, or hairy the yarn. When you crochet, on the other hand, the place where you insert the hook is part of the fabric you've already created, not ready and waiting on a hook or needle. If you're working with a textured yarn, it can be particularly tricky to figure out where to insert the hook. You may encounter another irritation when you crochet with yarns that have a very loose or soft twist: You're more likely to split these yarns. In spite of these potential pitfalls, you should feel free to use any yarn you choose: just remember that you might have to adjust a little in the process.

Easy Does It

Here are some tips that will help you avoid any problems when you're crocheting:

Soft twist yarns may split

- If you're using a mohair-type yarn, the hairy fibers often have a tendency to stick to each other, making it more difficult for you to pull the yarn through the loops. Try going up a hook size so that the loop is larger. Of course, you still have to stay on gauge, so check it again as you go along.

- Make a habit of keeping track by counting your stitches as you work a crochet pattern.
- To avoid splitting the yarn, try tightening up on your tension, so that you force the fibers closer together. Again, watch your gauge if you do this. Taking care to move the yarn to the shaft of the hook will help you avoid creating smaller stitches.

En~gauging matters

How many times have you heard this time-worn advice: Be sure to check your stitch and row gauges! Well, I'm here to tell you one more time. When you're working knit and crochet stitches on the same piece, it's especially important, because you'll have to make some adjustments. Let's say you're working with a sport-weight cotton yarn and the yarn label suggests that you use a US size 5 knitting needle to get six stitches to the inch and a size F crochet hook to get five stitches to the inch. (See page 187 for needle and hook sizes.) Even though you're using the same yarn for both the crochet and the knit sections, each crochet stitch uses up more space than a knit stitch, resulting in fewer stitches per inch when you're crocheting.

It can be just a little tricky marrying the techniques because of this difference in gauge. I've already figured out how to make the knitting stitches match to the crochet for the patterns in this book, so if you follow my suggestions for both knitting and crochet gauge, you won't have to worry much about this. It's good to understand the concept, though, so that you can confidently add crochet to favorite patterns from other sources. For example, when you use the same yarn to add a crochet edging to a knit garment, you need to pick up fewer stitches than those available along knit-

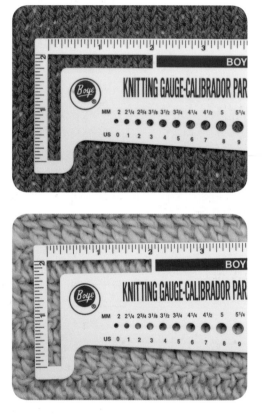

Counting stitches per inch in knitting (top) and crochet (bottom)

ted edges. If you're using a lighter-weight yarn, however, you might be able to use the same number of stitches for both. Picking up stitches is the procedure that causes most problems when blending the two techniques, and you'll find more advice on how to do it on page 20.

THE BEST OF BOTH WORLDS

As I've mentioned, both knitting and crochet have their strong points. In order to blend the two seamlessly (no pun intended), it's important to take advantage of the best characteristics of each. The knitters among you already value the qualities that knitted garments and home-decorating items offer, such as the lovely drape of the stockinette stitch and the wrist-hugging character of a knit 1, purl 1 rib. In the next few pages, I'm going to analyze some specific crochet techniques in order to demonstrate why I like to add these elements to my knitted designs.

On the Edge

Lacy Beaded Fingerless Gloves

Crochet is the ideal choice for an edging or trim. Knitting just can't compete with the flexibility and ease of crochet in this situation. Each crochet stitch is independent of the previous stitch, so you can readily move the hook up, down, and around whatever you're working on. In addition, working a crochet trim on your knitted piece helps keep the piece stable and prevent rolled edges. It's also a great way to add interest and color to a plain item with minimal effort.

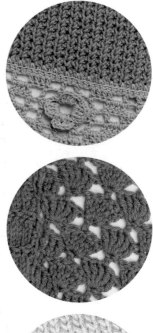

The Baby Washcloths (page 16) feature three very simple trims. The Elegant Placemat and Napkin Rings set (page 159) offers you an opportunity to show off your skills with a more complex edging. By adding a little beading to your trim, like that on these Lacy Beaded Fingerless Gloves (at left and page 29), you also add instant glamour.

The *shell stitch* is one that excels both as an edging and as a much larger part of a garment. It's one that I'm sure you've seen and admired many times for its rolling, scalloped edge. The "shell" is created by a simple repeat of stitches into one space. Its versatile nature allows you to use it to create an open look or a more closed fabric. The shell is also great when you need to create shaping, as you just drop off a shell here and there to create the needed effect.

Baby Washcloths

Baby will certainly look forward to bathtime with these soft, colorful washcloths. Knit them on the diagonal in oh-so-simple garter stitch with a sturdy, yet soft, cotton yarn, then add a sweet little crochet trim in one of three easy edgings. I worked mine with the same color trim as the knitted cloth, but you can have fun and mix it up, if you wish. These sweet little washcloths make a perfect baby shower gift that really shows how much you care.

Finished Measurements
6" (15 cm) square

Yarn
Rowan Handknit Cotton, 100% cotton,
   1.75 oz (50 g)/93 yds (85 m)
1 ball each color: #239 (icewater),
   #309 (celery), #251 (ecru)

Tools
Knit US #6 (4 mm) straight needles, or size
   you need to obtain correct gauge
Crochet Size F/5 (4 mm) crochet hook, or
   size you need to obtain correct gauge

Gauge
Knit 18 sts and 32 rows = 4" × 4"
   (10 cm × 10 cm) in Garter Stitch
Crochet 16 sc = 4" (10 cm)

Other Supplies
Large-eye yarn needle

Abbreviations
ch = chain
ch- = chained loop or chained space
dc = double crochet
K2tog = knit 2 together
sc = single crochet
yo = yarn over

Knitting the Washcloth

SET UP Using desired yarn color and straight needles, cast on 4 stitches. Knit 2 rows.	
ROW 1 K2, yo, knit to end of row.	
ROWS 2–32 Repeat Row 1. You now have 36 stitches.	
ROW 33 K1, K2tog, yo, K2tog, knit to end of row.	
ROWS 34–63 Repeat Row 33. You now have 4 stitches.	
LAST TWO ROWS Knit to end of row. Bind off all stitches.	

Crocheting the Edging Base

NOTE In this section, you will crochet a base for the edgings. For each washcloth, work the base around the entire edge and then finish with one of the three edgings. You can use the same or any one of the contrasting colors for the base and edging.

FIRST CORNER Using a crochet hook, join yarn into the first cast-on stitch. 1 sc into same stitch, 2 sc into next 2 stitches, 1 sc into next stitch.

FIRST EDGE 1 sc into every other row along first edge of the washcloth.

SECOND CORNER 3 sc into corner row.

SECOND EDGE 1 sc into every other row along second edge.

THIRD CORNER 1 sc into next stitch, 2 sc into next 2 stitches, 1 sc into next stitch.

THIRD EDGE 1 sc into every other row along third edge.

FOURTH CORNER 3 sc into corner row.

FOURTH EDGE 1 sc into every other row along fourth edge. Join with slip stitch to first sc. Draw yarn through to fasten off, and break yarn.

NOTE If you are using the same yarn for the edging, you do not need to fasten off.

Finish

Three Crochet Edgings

A   B   C

NOTE Choose one of the following edgings to complete the project.

SIMPLE EDGE (A) Join yarn to first sc beyond corner. Ch 5, * skip 2 sc, 1 sc in next sc, ch 3; repeat from * around edge of washcloth. Join with slip stitch to second chain of ch-5. Draw tail through last stitch to fasten off, then break yarn.

SHELL EDGE (B) Join yarn to first sc beyond corner. * 1 sc in same stitch, skip 1 stitch, 3 dc in next stitch, skip 1 stitch; repeat from * around edge of washcloth. Join with slip stitch to first sc. Draw tail through last stitch to fasten off, then break yarn.

PICOT EDGE (C) Join yarn to first sc beyond corner. * 1 sc in same stitch, ch 4, 1 sc into fourth chain from hook, sc in next stitch; repeat from * around edge of washcloth. Join with slip stitch to first sc. Draw tail through last stitch to fasten off, then break yarn.

Openwork and Lace Crochet

My project has a hole in it, and it's a good thing! You usually don't want to have holes in your fabric, of course, but because of the unique structure of crochet, you can achieve the most wonderful and unusual effects when you purposely work a series of "holes." Crochet has the strength to hold up even when you work large, consecutive holes to create a very lacy, open effect. This technique is sometimes referred to as *filet crochet*. You may have seen it on edges or inserts in vintage tablecloths and pillowcases. Depending on how you place the holes, the whole piece can be lacy and open or you can eliminate some of the holes for more-opaque sections in the fabric.

I played on this strength of crochet to achieve an open fabric, even with the rather heavy yarn I used for the Openwork V-Neck Cardigan (page 121). The structure of the crochet stitch keeps stretch and sag to a minimum, in spite of the openness of the pattern.

Granny Squares and Motifs

Granny squares, which are sometimes worked as hexagons or triangles as well as squares or rectangles, and the many-faceted, often sculptural pieces that I call *motifs* are unique to crochet. Grannies and motifs are delightfully portable, as you work on only one at a time. Both can be used to create colorful interest on a knitted piece.

The familiar, traditional "granny" is one of my favorite elements, and I used it for the old-fashioned Granny-Square Afghan with Wide Knitted Border (page 145), updated with a gracefully knitted edge. You can work grannies in a number of stitch variations to change the look dramatically, as, for example, in the Back-to-School Backpack (page 67) and the Peek-a-Boo Pillows (page 151).

Use motifs to embellish sweaters, hats, purses, and even pillows as lavishly as you want. You can also work motifs right into the structure of the fabric, as I did in the Ice-Blue Openwork Scarf shown (page 47).

I especially love sculptural embellishments, and I love to work them in crochet. Because crochet is so malleable, it's perfect for making three-dimensional shapes. Flower motifs are particularly easy to make in crochet, and you'll find a variety of crocheted flowers in this book (see pages 42, 52, 62, 96, and 168). I hope you'll be inspired to try the different versions and use them liberally. Notice the bobble at the center of the flowers on the flowered scarf. The bobble is another simple decoration. Use it in combination with other embellishments, or let it be the star accent, like the "cherries" on the Berries and Buttons Sweater (page 135).

Getting Attached

When you attach your embellishments, take a minute to consider what yarn or thread is best for the situation. If your stitches will show, as in the Garland-of-Flowers Scarf, be sure to use the same yarn you used to knit the scarf. Whatever you choose, it's important to sew it on securely, so it will stay put.

A large-eye yarn needle is perfect for this task, as you'll be able to thread most weights of yarn through the eye fairly easily. Before you begin to sew the embellishment in place, weave in any loose ends, so that they're out of sight and out of your way. (If the yarn is the right color, you may be able to use the tail that you fastened off with as

your sewing thread.) Pick up only one or two strands of yarn from the embellishment and the base piece for each stitch, weaving back and forth between the two. If you want your flower to stand away from the base fabric a bit, attach the petals only about halfway to their tips.

The easiest way to attach a bobble is to pull one long tail through one side of a stitch of the base and the other tail through the other side of the stitch, then thread the tails through a needle, one by one, and catch a few stitches to secure the bobble in place. Don't sew the bobble on too tight, or it will flatten.

When attaching a flower, allow the petals to stand free.

To attach a bobble, draw both tails to wrong side and thread through needle.

It's All in the Technique

To help you expand your arsenal of skills, I'd like to offer a few tips on how to pick up knit stitches for the crochet section of a project, as well as how to pick up crochet stitches in order to begin knitting. I'll also give you some information about how to finish and assemble your projects.

Picking Up Knit Stitches to Crochet

I've always found that picking up stitches with a crochet hook is much easier than doing it with a knitting needle. In fact, many knitters use a crochet hook to pick up their knitting stitches for transfer to the needle or to repair dropped stitches. When you pick up stitches along a row to crochet or knit, you may have to adjust by either skipping rows or working two rows together as needed to get the right number of stitches. This is because with most yarns and gauges you'll get more rows than stitches per inch in both knitting and crochet. Similarly, when you pick up stitches to crochet along a cast-on or cast-off edge, you'll also need fewer crochet stitches per inch than are available in the knit stitches. Compensate by either skipping stitches or working two together as needed to get a smooth edge. I've spelled this out in each of the patterns, but I mention it here so you won't be surprised when you encounter it.

To pick up for an edge, insert the crochet hook through both "legs" of the knit stitch, whether you're working along the cast-on or cast-off stitches or along a row.

When picking up along a side edge of a knitted piece, you may need to skip every other row.

When picking up along a top edge of a knitted piece, compensate as needed: here, I picked up 2 stitches in a row then skipped one.

Picking Up

For a more finished, professional look it pays to plan ahead for any shaping while you're working the knit portion of your project: Make the increases and decreases on the second or third stitches in from the edge. This leaves you a full stitch to use when picking up along rows, so you get a neater, flatter edge.

Picking Up Crochet Stitches to Knit

When you study the top of a crochet stitch, you'll notice that it looks very similar to a bound-off knit stitch. Although this makes it easy to pick up the crochet stitches with a knitting needle, I actually prefer using a crochet hook to pick them up and then transfer them to my needle.

It's more of a challenge to pick up stitches along an open-work pattern or along the row edge of a crochet item. Because the structure of the crochet stitch varies according to the pattern you're following, it's difficult to give specific advice on how to get around the challenge. In general, however, I like to insert my hook between two stitches on the edge in order to get a firm connection.

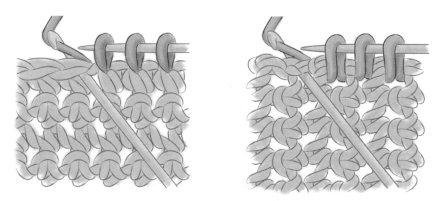

When picking up along either a top edge (left) or a side edge (right), insert your hook between two stitches for a firm connection.

Finishing Touches

I have to confess that my least favorite part of any project is the finishing. You would think that being so close to the end, I would be excited to have the piece done and that I would hurry through this part, but I don't. For me the finishing is a bit anti-climactic. As I'm making the piece, I can see it evolve and that's exciting, but once I get to the finishing, it becomes just a little tedious.

Much of the finishing process is the same whether the item is knitted or crocheted: You weave in ends, block the pieces, then sew them together. It's the sewing together that can be a little tricky. As I've mentioned, the top of a crochet stitch resembles a stitch on a bound-off knit edge, but there's usually a difference in the number of stitches per inch in the crocheted and knitted pieces. The best way to deal with this is to count the rows and stitches and then calculate how to align them with each other. For instance, let's say you have a knitted front and a crocheted back that you want to sew together at the shoulder. In this case, you're matching the tops of both crochet and knit stitches. Here's an example of the procedure to follow:

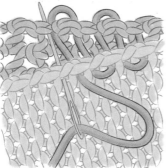

To sew a knitted piece to a crocheted piece, calculate the number of stitches (top) or rows (bottom) in each piece and distribute them accordingly.

Shoulder width = 6"
Knit gauge = 5 stitches per inch (30 stitches per 6")
Crochet gauge = 4 stitches per inch (24 stitches per 6")
You have six more stitches on the knit edge than on the crochet edge (30 − 24 = 6).
To determine how to distribute them evenly over the width of the shoulder, divide 30 by 6: You need to work 2 stitches together every 5 stitches across the knit edge. Here's how: Match up and sew together 3 stitches, then sew the next 2 knit stitches to the next crochet stitch. Continue in this way across the seam.

Although when you read the math, it may seem confusing, once you actually put it into practice, you'll get the hang of it and find it's really very easy. Follow the same procedure when you're sewing the side edge of a crocheted piece to the side edge of a knit piece (the row edges), as well as when you're sewing a side edge to a top or bottom edge (a row edge to the top of stitches).

Get on the Bandwagon

Now that you're versed in the fine art of combining knitting and crochet, you may find that you want to incorporate crochet into any number of projects. A crochet button band is an easy way to add a little texture and detailing to a plain (or even a fancy!) knit piece. Working buttonholes into the button band is a snap, and feel free to add a little picot edge to complete the effect. Creating crochet buttons is also a simple procedure and a great way to decorate a garment with interesting, matching buttons. You may want to incorporate a few beads into your buttons to give them even more flair. (See Button, Button, Who's Got the Button on page 24.)

I like to work the basic button band in single crochet. You can also use half double or double crochet, but it may be too open and without enough structure. You can always dress up the single-crochet base with more-complex stitches for the last row, if you want.

To work the button band, with right side facing you, pick up stitches along the edge of the button side (the left front for women and the right front for men). Work one row of single crochet, then chain 1, turn, and work another row of single crochet back down the stitches. Two rows are enough for most bands, but depending on the weight of the yarn, you may need another row or two. Patterns indicate how many rows to work, but if you're designing your own band, use your judgment as to how wide it should be.

A buttonhole created by chain 1, skip 1 along a single crochet base.

To work the buttonhole side of the band, first space pins evenly along the just-completed button band to mark where you want each button. As you work the buttonhole band, you will need to compare measurements to the button band to determine the placement of each buttonhole. With the right side facing you, join the yarn and pick up stitches in the same manner as before. Work one row of single crochet, chain 1, and turn. On the second row, single crochet until you are opposite the first point marked on the button band; chain 1, skip 1 stitch (you've created the buttonhole), and then continue single crochet until you're opposite the next marked spot; repeat chain 1, skip 1 stitch. Continue in this way until you reach the end of the band. Note: Always make the top and bottom buttonholes at least a stitch or two away from the top or bottom edge. You should then work one more row after the buttonhole.

Button, Button, Who's Got the Button?

Over the years, I've seen many ways to create crocheted buttons. I'm going to show you a basic, simple form, but it's by no means the only way to do it. Because a button has to stand up to endless shoving and pushing in and out of a buttonhole, it's important to consider the structure of the stitch. You can usually work with the same size hook that you used for the rest of the garment, but if you're making a button for something you didn't knit or crochet, or the garment you worked on is very loosely crocheted, you might want to experiment and go down a hook size, just to make sure the stitches are tight enough.

A Small Crocheted Button

SET UP Chain 2, leaving a yarn tail of about 6 inches.

ROUND 1 8 sc in second chain from hook. Slip stitch into first sc.

ROUND 2 Ch 1; * draw up a loop in first sc; draw up a loop in next sc; yarn over hook and draw through all three loops on hook; repeat from * to end (all 8 sc in Round 1 are now worked); slip stitch in first sc to complete round. End by drawing a 6" yarn tail through the last stitch. Thread tail through a large-eye needle and weave it through stitches; pull tight to close.

To attach the button to the piece, pull both tails through to the wrong side and fasten off (see page 19).

A Large Crocheted Button

SET UP Chain 2, leaving a yarn tail of about 6 inches.

ROUND 1 8 sc in second chain from hook. Slip stitch into first sc.

ROUND 2 Ch 1, * 1 sc into first stitch and 2 sc into next stitch; repeat from * around, ending with a slip stitch into first sc. (12 sts)

ROUND 3 Repeat Round 2. (18 sts)

ROUND 4 Chain 1; * draw up a loop in first sc; draw up a loop in next sc; yarn over hook and draw through all three loops on hook; repeat from * to end (all 18 sc in Round 3 are now worked); slip stitch in first sc to complete round. End by drawing a 6" yarn tail through the last stitch. Thread tail through a large-eye needle and weave it through stitches; pull tight to close. Attach buttons in the same way as described for the Small Crocheted Button (at left).

Beaded Buttons

To add some sizzle to a button, thread beads onto the yarn and pull them up as you work.

TIP: Depending on the weight of the yarn and the size of the beads, it may be difficult to thread them onto the yarn. To overcome this problem, thread a regular sewing needle with a 10-inch length of thread, line up the thread ends, and knot them together. Draw the end of the yarn through the two threads, leaving about 6 inches of the yarn hanging down. Thread a bead onto the needle, draw it down the thread and then down onto the yarn.

CHAPTER 1

Accessorize!

Lacy Beaded Fingerless Gloves

Here's a way to make the ordinary extraordinary with just a few extra steps. A simple but elegant knitted lace stitch graces the front of the glove, while the flip side is in easy stockinette stitch. The bonus here is the easy-to-crochet trim with a little brilliant beading. This is a perfect project to tackle if you've never beaded before — not too overwhelming, with a lot of bang for the buck. You'll be so hooked that you'll want these gloves in a rainbow of colors.

Sizes and Finished Measurements
Small/Medium 7" × 6"
  (17.5 cm × 15 cm)
Medium/Large 8" × 6½"
  (20 cm × 16.25 cm)

Yarn
Nashua Handknits, June, 100% microfiber,
  2 oz (56 gm)/150 yds (132 m)
1 ball #0003 (rose)

Tools
Knit US #6 (4 mm) straight needles, or size
  you need to obtain correct gauge
Crochet Size E/4 (3.5 mm) crochet hook, or
  size you need to obtain correct gauge

Gauge
Knit 22 sts and 28 rows = 4" × 4"
  (10 cm × 10 cm) in Stockinette Stitch
Crochet 20 sc = 4" (10 cm)

Other Supplies
Large-eye yarn needle
1 package Westrim gold beads, #4997

Abbreviations
ch = chain (verb)
ch- = chained loop or chained space
K2tog = knit 2 together
Psso = pass slipped stitch over
sc = single crochet
St st = stockinette stitch
yo = yarn over

Knitting the Left Glove

	[S/M]		[M/L]
SET UP Using straight needles, cast on	38 sts	•	44 sts
STARTER ROW Purl to end of row.			
ROW 1 (RIGHT SIDE) Knit	6 sts	•	8 sts
then K2tog, K2, yo, K1, yo, K5, slip 1, K1, psso, end knit	20 sts	•	24 sts
ROWS 2, 4, 6, 8, 10, AND 12 Purl to end of row.			
ROW 3 Knit	6 sts	•	8 sts
then K2tog, K1, yo, K3, yo, K4, slip 1, K1, psso, end knit	20 sts	•	24 sts
ROW 5 Knit	6 sts	•	8 sts
then K2tog, yo, K5, yo, K3, slip 1, K1, psso, end knit	20 sts	•	24 sts
ROW 7 Knit	6 sts	•	8 sts
then K2tog, K5, yo, K1, yo, K2, slip 1, K1, psso, end knit	20 sts	•	24 sts
ROW 9 Knit	6 sts	•	8 sts
then K2tog, K4, yo, K3, yo, K1, slip 1, K1, psso, end knit	20 sts	•	24 sts
ROW 11 Knit	6 sts	•	8 sts
then K2tog, K3, yo, K5, yo, slip 1, K1, psso, end knit	20 sts	•	24 sts
NEXT ROWS Repeat Rows 1–12	once more	•	once more
Medium/Large only Repeat rows 1–6		•	once more
Bind off on the last purl row.			

Crocheting the Edging

Incorporating a bead in the edging

SET UP For Small/Medium, string 54 beads on yarn; for Medium/Large, string 60 beads on yarn.

NOTE The tip of the yarn may become dirty or frayed during the bead stringing. Be sure to clip off the damaged part before continuing.

STARTER ROW Using crochet hook, join yarn to the lower right edge of glove. With wrong side of glove facing you, * 1 sc in first stitch, ch 1, skip 1; repeat from * across edge. Ch 2, turn.

ROW 1 (RIGHT SIDE) * Slide up bead against work, ch 2, 1 sc in ch-1 space; repeat from * across, ending 1 sc in ch-1 space; ch 4, turn.

ROW 2 * 1 sc in sc, ch 3; repeat from * across, ending 1 sc in last sc. Ch 2, turn.

ROW 3 * Slide bead against work, ch 2, 1 sc into ch-3 space, ch 1; repeat from * across, ending 1 sc in second chain of ch-4. Draw yarn through last stitch to fasten off, then break yarn.

Knitting the Right Glove

	[S/M]		[M/L]
SET UP Using straight needles, cast on	38 sts	•	44 sts
STARTER ROW Purl to end of row.			
ROW 1 (RIGHT SIDE) Knit	20 sts	•	24 sts
then K2tog, K2, yo, K1, yo, K5, slip 1, K1, psso, end knit	6 sts	•	8 sts
ROWS 2, 4, 6, 8, 10, AND 12 Purl to end of row.			
ROW 3 Knit	20 sts	•	24 sts
then K2tog, K1, yo, K3, yo, K4, slip 1, K1, psso, end knit	6 sts	•	8 sts

KNITTING THE RIGHT GLOVE (continued)

	[S/M]		[M/L]
ROW 5 Knit	20 sts	•	24 sts
then K2tog, yo, K5, yo, K3, slip 1, K1, psso, end knit	6 sts	•	8 sts
ROW 7 Knit	20 sts	•	24 sts
then K2tog, K5, yo, K1, yo, K2, slip 1, K1, psso, end knit	6 sts	•	8 sts
ROW 9 Knit	20 sts	•	24 sts
then K2tog, K4, yo, K3, yo, K1, slip 1, K1, psso, end knit	6 sts	•	8 sts
ROW 11 Knit	20 sts	•	24 sts
then K2tog, K3, yo, K5, yo, slip 1, K1, psso, end knit	6 sts	•	8 sts
NEXT ROWS Repeat Rows 1–12	once more	•	once more
Medium/Large only Repeat Rows 1–6		•	once more
BIND OFF on the last purl row.			
Crochet the edging as for the Left Glove.			

Crocheting Top Edge

Using crochet hook, join yarn to top left edge of glove. With wrong side of glove facing you, ch 2, * slide a bead against work, ch 1, skip 1 stitch, 1 sc in back loop only of next stitch; repeat from * across, ending 1 sc. Draw yarn through last stitch to fasten off, then break yarn.

Repeat Edging on other glove.

Finish

	[S/M]	[M/L]
① Using yarn needle, sew side seam from top edge for 1" (2.5 cm). For thumb hole, leave open for	1½" (3.75 cm)	1½" (3.75 cm)

② Sew remainder of seam below thumb hole.

③ With crochet hook, join yarn at thumb opening. * 1 sc, ch 1, skip 2; repeat from * around opening. End with slip stitch in first sc. Draw yarn through last stitch to fasten off, then break yarn.

FINISH the second glove in same manner.

Cozy Hat & Arm Warmers

It's hard to tell which is knit and which is crochet in these perfectly blended pieces. Create a warm and wonderful hat and matching gauntlets in a matter of hours switching between the knit rib and the crochet bobbles. Worked in a warm, textured wool that is sure to chase off the winter chill!

Finished Measurements
Hat 18" (45 cm) circumference;
   8" (20 cm) length
Gauntlets 4" (10 cm) circumference;
   6" (15 cm) length

Yarn
Classic Elite Bazic, 100% Superwash wool,
   1.75 oz (50 g)/65 yds (59 m)
   4 balls # 2958 Barn Red

Tools
Knit US #8 (5 mm) straight needles, or size
   you need to obtain correct gauge
Crochet Size H/8 (5 mm) crochet hook, or
   size you need to obtain correct gauge

Gauge
Knit 18 sts and 24 rows = 4" × 4"
   (10 cm × 10 cm) in Knit Pattern Stitch
Crochet 12 sts and 15 rows = 4" × 4"
   (10 cm × 10 cm) in Crochet Pattern Stitch

Other Supplies
Large-eye yarn needle

Abbreviations
ch = chain (verb)
ch- = chained loop or chained space
hdc = half double crochet
sc = single crochet
tr = treble crochet

Pattern Stitches

Knit Pattern Stitch

ROW 1 (RIGHT SIDE) * K2, P2; repeat from * to end of row.

ROW 2 * P2, K2; repeat from * to end of row.

ROW 3 * P2, K2; repeat from * to end of row.

ROW 4 * K2, P2; repeat from * to end of row.

Crochet Pattern Stitch

ROW 1 1 sc, * 1 tr, 1 sc; repeat from * to end of row, ch 3 (counts as hdc, ch 1), turn.

ROW 2 Skip 2 stitches, * work 1 hdc in sc, ch 1, skip 1; repeat from * to end of row, ending 1 hdc, ch 1, turn.

ROW 3 * 1 sc in hdc, 1 tr in ch-1 space; repeat from * to end of row, ending with 1 sc, ch 3, turn.

Repeat Rows 2 and 3 for Crochet Pattern Stitch.

Knitting the Hat

SET UP Using straight needles, cast on 80 sts.

ROWS 1–20 Work Rows 1–4 of Knit Pattern Stitch five times, or until piece measures 5" (12.5 cm).

BIND OFF in pattern.

Crocheting the Hat Band

SET UP Using crochet hook, join yarn to cast-on edge.

STARTER ROW * 1 sc in first stitch, 1 sc in next stitch, insert hook into next 2 stitches and work 1 sc (1 decrease made); repeat from * to end of row, ch 1, turn. *You now have 60 sc.*

ROW 1 Work Row 1 of Crochet Pattern Stitch.

ROWS 2–9 Work Rows 2 and 3 of Crochet Pattern Stitch 4 times.

Draw yarn through to fasten off, and break yarn.

Using yarn needle, sew side seam. Weave a 6" (15 cm) length of yarn through bound-off knit stitches and pull snug to shape top of hat. Tie off yarn.

Knitting the Arm Warmers Ribbing

SET UP Using straight needles, cast on 40 stitches.

ROW 1 * K2, P2; repeat from * to end of row.

ROW 2 * P2, K2; repeat from * to end of row.

ROWS 3–16 Repeat Rows 1 and 2 seven times, or until piece measures 4" (10 cm).

BIND OFF in ribbing.

Crocheting the Arm Warmers Trim

SET UP Using crochet hook, join yarn to first stitch of bound-off row.

STARTER ROW * 1 sc in first stitch, 1 sc in next stitch, insert hook into next 2 stitches and work 1 sc (1 decrease made); repeat from * to end of row. *You now have 30 sc.*

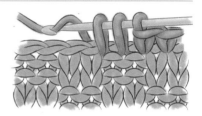

Decrease by working 1 sc in 2 stitches

ROW 1 Work Row 1 of Crochet Pattern Stitch.

ROWS 2–7 Work Rows 2 and 3 of Crochet Pattern Stitch 3 times. Break off yarn.

Finish

1 Using yarn needle, sew side seam.

2 Make another arm warmer to match.

Top It Off

Hats are no longer just something to pull on your head to keep you warm or to ward off a bad-hair day. They have become the ultimate fashion accessory. Make this easy-knit chapeau in a variety of colors. I chose a warm teal blue, great for every mood and style. Spice up the cap with creative and colorful crochet motifs and just a hint of crochet around the edge.

Finished Measurements
22" × 7" (55 cm × 17.5 cm)

Yarn
Rowan Julia, 25% kid mohair/25% alpaca/50% lambs wool, 1.75 oz (50 g)/93 yd (85 m)
MC = 1 ball #6396 Deep Sea Blue
CC = 1 ball #3961 Lady's Mantle

Tools
Knit US #7 (4.5 mm) straight needles, or size you need to obtain correct gauge
Crochet Size H/8 (5 mm) crochet hook, or size you need to obtain correct gauge

Gauge
Knit 12 sts and 12 rows = 4" × 4" (10 cm × 10 cm) in Knit Pattern Stitch
Crochet 14 sts and 16 rows = 4" × 4" (10 cm × 10 cm) in sc

Other Supplies
Large-eye yarn needle

Abbreviations
CC = contrasting color
ch = chain (verb)
ch- = chained loop or chained space
dc = double crochet
hdc = half double crochet
K2tog = knit 2 together
MC = main color
sc = single crochet
yo = yarn over

Pattern Stitches

Knit Pattern Stitch

ROW 1 * K2tog, yo; repeat from * to last stitch, K1.

ROWS 2 AND 3 Knit to end of row.

Crochet Flower Pattern

STARTER ROUND Ch 4, join with slip stitch to form ring.

ROUND 1 Ch 4 (counts as 1 dc and ch 1), * 1 dc, ch 1; repeat from * 9 more times. Join with slip stitch to third ch of ch-4. Draw yarn through last stitch to fasten off, then break yarn.

ROUND 2 Join yarn in any ch-2 space, ch 4 (counts as 1 sc and ch 3), * 1 sc in ch-2 sp, ch 3; repeat from * around. End with slip stitch to first ch of ch-3. Draw yarn through last stitch to fasten off, then break yarn.

Knitting the Crown

SET UP Using MC and straight needles, cast on 67 sts.

FIRST ROWS Work Rows 1–3 of Knit Pattern Stitch until it measures 4" (10 cm).

End on Row 2 and ready to begin Row 3.

NEXT ROW (1ST DECREASE ROW) * K6, K2tog; repeat from * to last stitch, K1.

NEXT 2 ROWS Repeat Rows 1 and 2 of Knit Pattern Stitch.

NEXT ROW (2ND DECREASE ROW) * K5, K2tog; repeat from * to last stitch, K1.

NEXT 2 ROWS Repeat Rows 1 and 2 of Knit Pattern Stitch.

NEXT ROW (3RD DECREASE ROW) * K4, K2tog; repeat from * to last stitch, K1.

NEXT 2 ROWS Repeat Rows 1 and 2 of Knit Pattern Stitch.

NEXT ROW (4TH DECREASE ROW) * K3, K2tog; repeat from * to last stitch, K1.

NEXT 2 ROWS Repeat Rows 1 and 2 of Knit Pattern Stitch.

NEXT ROW (5TH DECREASE ROW) * K2, K2tog; repeat from * to last stitch, K1.

NEXT 2 ROWS Repeat Rows 1 and 2 of Knit Pattern Stitch.

NEXT ROW (6TH DECREASE ROW) * K1, K2tog; repeat from * to last stitch, K1.

NEXT 2 ROWS Repeat Rows 1 and 2 of Knit Pattern Stitch.

NEXT ROW (7TH DECREASE ROW) * K2tog; repeat from * to last stitch, K1.

NEXT 2 ROWS Repeat Rows 1 and 2 of Knit Pattern Stitch.

BIND OFF all stitches, leaving a long tail to sew seam. Thread yarn through yarn needle. Pull together the top stitches and sew seam.

Crocheting the Edging

SET UP Using MC and crochet hook, join yarn to cast-on edge of hat.

STARTER ROUND Work 1 sc in each stitch to end of row. Change to CC. You now have 67 sc.

ROUND 1 Work (1 sc in each sc) 11 times, (insert hook through next 2 stitches, yo, pull yarn through all loops on hook — 1 decrease made). * (1 sc in each sc) 21 times, decrease 1; repeat from * one more time. End (1 sc in each sc) 11 times. You now have 64 sc.

Ch 4 (counts as 1 hdc and ch 2), turn.

ROUND 2 Skip 1, * 1 hdc in next sc, ch 2, skip 1; repeat from * around. Join last ch-2 with slip stitch to second ch of ch-4. Ch 2, turn.

ROUND 3 * Work 3 dc in first ch-2 space, 1 sc in next ch-2 space; repeat from * around. End with slip stitch to top of ch-2. Break off yarn.

Crocheting the Flowers

NOTE Refer to Crochet Flower Pattern.

FLOWER 1 Using CC and crochet hook, make one flower.

FLOWER 2 Using CC and crochet hook, work Starter Round and Round 1. Change to MC for Round 2.

FLOWER 3 Using MC and crochet hook, work Starter Round and Round 1. Change to CC for Round 2.

Finish

Use MC and yarn needle to tack flowers to front of hat as shown below. (See page 19 for sewing on flowers.)

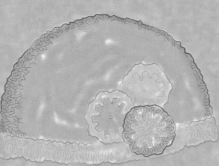

Ice-Blue Openwork Scarf

Alternating between knitting and crochet will keep you interested as you create this unique scarf. Work the bands of knitting in simple garter stitch with a few dropped stitches thrown in, then attach the playful crochet accents once the knitting is done. This scarf will surely have your friends begging for one and put you on a creative pedestal.

Finished Measurements
5 ¾" × 86" (14 cm × 2 m)

Yarn
Classic Elite Provence, 100% cotton,
   3.5 oz (100 g)/93 yds (85 m)
MC = 1 skein #2621 Herbal Sage
CC = 1 skein #2607 Clear Blue Sky

Tools
Knit US #10 (6 mm) straight needles, or
   size you need to obtain correct gauge
Crochet Size G/6 (4.25 mm) crochet hook,
   or size you need to obtain correct gauge

Gauge
Knit 14 sts and 24 rows = 4" × 4"
   (10 cm × 10 cm) in Garter Stitch
Crochet 1 motif = 4" (10 cm)

Other Supplies
Large-eye yarn needle

Abbreviations
CC = contrasting color
ch = chain (verb)
ch- = chained loop or chained space
dc = double crochet
hdc = half double crochet
MC = main color
sc = single crochet

Pattern Stitches

Knit Panel Pattern Stitch

ROW 1 * K1, wrap yarn around needle twice; repeat from *, end K1.

ROW 2 * K1, drop wrapped stitches; repeat from *, end K1.

ROW 3 Knit to end of row.

ROWS 4–6 Repeat Rows 1–3.

ROWS 7–16 Knit to end of row.

ROWS 17–22 Repeat Rows 1–6.

Crochet Motif Pattern Stitch

STARTER ROUND Ch 5, join with slip stitch to form ring.

ROUND 1 Ch 6 (counts as 1 dc and ch 3), * 1 dc into ring, ch 3; repeat from * four more times, end with slip stitch into third chain of ch-6. Draw the yarn through to fasten off, then break yarn.

ROUND 2 Join yarn into any ch-3 space, ch 6 (counts as 1 sc and ch 5), * 1 sc into next space, ch 5; repeat from * four more times, end with slip stitch into first sc. Draw yarn through to fasten off, then break yarn.

ROUND 3 * Work (1 sc, 1 hdc, 1 dc, ch-3, slip stitch into third ch of ch-3, 1 dc, 1 hdc, 1 sc) into each ch-5 space, end with slip stitch into first sc. Draw the yarn through to fasten off, then break yarn.

Knitting the Garter Stitch Panels

SET UP Using MC and straight needles, cast on 20 stitches.

ROWS 1–22 Work Rows 1–22 of Knit Panel Pattern Stitch.

Bind off. Make 6 more exactly the same.

then

Crocheting the Motifs

With crochet hook, work Crochet Motif Pattern Stitch, using MC for Starter Round and Rounds 1 and 2, and CC for Round 3.

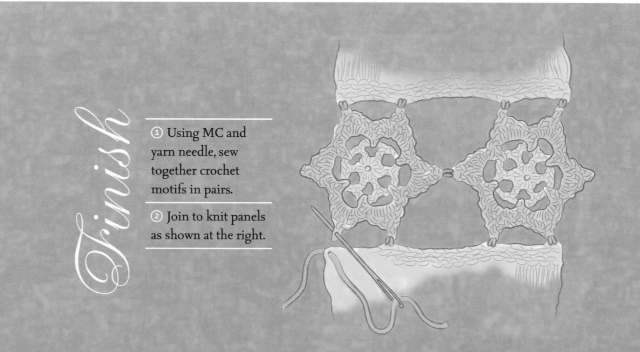

① Using MC and yarn needle, sew together crochet motifs in pairs.

② Join to knit panels as shown at the right.

Garland-of-Flowers Scarf

A riot of flowers blooming around your neck is sure to turn the gloomiest day into spring. Big and blowsy crochet flowers enliven the ends of this very basic garter-stitch scarf. For a little extra springtime fun, make the flowers in a bunch of different colors — your own inspired spring bouquet!

Finished Measurements
3" × 38" (7.5 cm × 1 m), plus ties

Yarn
Classic Elite Bazic, 100% superwash wool,
   1.75 oz (50 g)/65 yds (60 m)
MC = 2 balls #2961 Carnation
CA = 1 ball #2958 Barn Red
CB = 1 ball #2955 Sun Opal
CC = 1 ball #2919 Impatiens
CD = 1 ball #2902 Wintergreen

Tools
Knit US #9 (5.5 mm) straight needles, or
   size you need to obtain correct gauge
Crochet Size H/8 (5 mm) crochet hook, or
   size you need to obtain correct gauge

Gauge
Knit 14 sts and 20 rows = 4" × 4"
   (10 cm × 10 cm) in Garter Stitch
Crochet 12 sts and 15 rows = 4" × 4"
   (10 cm × 10 cm) in sc

Other Supplies
Large-eye yarn needle

Abbreviations
CA = contrasting color A
CB = contrasting color B
CC = contrasting color C
CD = contrasting color D
ch = chain (verb)
ch- = chained loop or chained space
dc = double crochet
dtr = double treble crochet
hdc = half double crochet
K2tog = knit 2 together
MC = main color
sc = single crochet
tr = treble crochet
yo = yarn over

Pattern Stitches

Flower Pattern Stitch

SET UP Ch 4, join with slip stitch to form a ring, ch 1.

ROUND 1 Work 10 hdc into ring.

ROUND 2 Ch 2 (counts as 1 hdc), 1 hdc into base of ch-2, * 2 hdc into next hdc; repeat from * all around. *You now have* 20 hdc.

ROUND 3 Inserting hook into front loop of stitches only, * ch 3, 1 tr into base of ch-3, (2 tr into next hdc) twice, (1 tr, ch 3, slip stitch) into next hdc, slip stitch into next hdc; repeat from * four more times. Break off yarn. *You now have* 5 small petals.

ROUND 4 Join yarn into back loop of any center tr of one petal. Inserting hook into back loop of Round-3 stitches only, * ch 3, 1 dtr into base of ch, (2 dtr into next tr) twice, (1 dtr, ch 3, slip stitch) into next hdc, slip stitch into next hdc; repeat from * four more times. Draw yarn through to fasten off, then break yarn. *You now have* 5 large petals.

ROUND 5 Join yarn into any Round-1 hdc on front of work, (ch 3, sc) into each stitch in round, ending with slip stitch into base of ch-3. Draw yarn through to fasten off, and break yarn. *You now have* center ruffle.

BOBBLE Ch 3, * yo, insert hook into third chain from hook and draw up a loop, yo, draw through 2 loops on hook; repeat from * three more times, yo and draw through all 5 loops on hook. *You now have* 1 bobble.

Draw yarn through to fasten off, and leaving a long tail for sewing, break yarn. Use yarn needle to sew bobble to center of flower.

Knitting the Scarf Base

SET UP Using MC and straight needles, cast on 3 sts.

STARTER ROWS Knit 2 rows.

ROWS 1 AND 2 K1, increase 1, knit to end of row. *You now have 5 sts.*

ROWS 3 AND 4 Knit to end of row.

ROWS 5–16 Repeat Rows 1–4 three more times. *You now have 11 sts.*

NEXT ROWS Knit every row until piece measures 23½" (59 cm).

NEXT 2 ROWS K1, K2tog, knit to end of row. *You now have 9 sts.*

NEXT 2 ROWS Knit to end of row.

Repeat last 4 rows three more times. *You now have 3 sts.*

Bind off.

Crocheting the Flowers

Refer to Flower Pattern Stitch and the color notes below to make Flowers 1–7. See the diagram for flower placement on the scarf.

NOTE *The smaller flowers omit Round 4 of the Flower Pattern Stitch.*

Flower 1

Using CA, work Rounds 1–4.

Using CC, work Round 5.

Using CD, make and attach bobble.

Flower 2

Using MC, work Rounds 1–4.

Using CC, work Round 5.

Using CD, make and attach bobble.

Flower 3

Using CB, work Rounds 1–4.

Using CC, work Round 5.

Using CD, make and attach bobble.

Flower 4

Using CA, work Rounds 1–3.

Using CB, work Round 4.

Using CC, work Round 5.

Using CD, make and attach bobble.

Flower 5

Using MC, work Rounds 1–3. (Omit Round 4.)

Using CC, work Round 5.

Using CD, make and attach bobble.

Flower 6

Using CA, work Rounds 1–3. (Omit Round 4.)

Using CC, work Round 5.

Using CD, make and attach bobble.

Flower 7

Using CB, work Rounds 1–3. (Omit Round 4.)

Using CC, work Round 5.

Using CD, make and attach bobble.

Ties

Using CD and crochet hook, make a chain 14" (35 cm) long. Work 1 sc in each chain. Draw yarn through to fasten off, then break yarn. Make second tie 15" (37.5 cm) long.

Leaves

SET UP Using CD and crochet hook, ch 10.

① Insert hook in second chain from hook, 1 sc, 1 sc in next ch, (1 hdc in next ch) three times, (1 dc in next ch) three times, 3 tr in last ch; continuing down other side of chain, work (1 dc in next ch) three times, (1 hdc in next ch) three times, (1 sc in next ch) twice.

② Draw yarn through to fasten off, and leaving a long tail for attaching the leaves to the ties, break yarn.

③ Make 7 identical leaves.

Finish

Using matching yarn and yarn needle, sew flowers to scarf at each end. Sew ties to ends of scarf. Sew leaves to ties.

Over-the-Shoulder Opera Purse

Going out on the town with this dazzling shoulder bag, even if it's not exactly the opera, will make you feel like it could be. The "not-so-basic" granny square on the flap is worked in a glittering suede yarn, while the body of the bag is knit in a snug slip stitch. The perfect size for all those little necessities on a night on the town.

Finished Measurements
5"(12.5 cm) square, plus shoulder strap

Yarn
Berroco Suede Delux, 85% nylon/10% rayon/5% polyester, 1¾ oz (50g)/ 100 yds (92 m)
MC = 2 balls #1999 Zorro Silver (black)
CC = 1 ball #3901 Dale Evans (white)

Tools
Knit US #9 (5.5 mm) straight needles, or size you need to obtain correct gauge
Crochet Size G/6 (4 mm) crochet hook, or size you need to obtain correct gauge

Gauge
Knit 22 sts and 36 rows = 4" × 4" (10 cm × 10 cm) in Slip Stitch Pattern Stitch
Crochet 1 square = 5" × 5" (12.5 cm × 12.5 cm)

Other Supplies
Large-eye yarn needle
Magnetic snap

Abbreviations
CC = contrasting color
ch = chain (verb)
ch- = chained loop or chained space
dc = double crochet
MC = main color
sc = single crochet
tr = treble crochet

Pattern Stitches

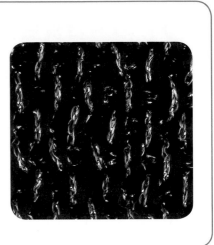

Slip Stitch Pattern Stitch

ROW 1 * K1, move yarn to front, slip 1 purlwise, move yarn to back; repeat from * to end of row.

ROW 2 * P1, move yarn to back, slip 1 purlwise, move yarn to front; repeat from * to end of row.

Knitting the Purse

SET UP Using MC and straight needles, cast on 28 sts.

ROW 1 Work Row 1 of Slip Stitch Pattern Stitch.

ROW 2 Work Row 2 of Slip Stitch Pattern Stitch.

Repeat Rows 1 and 2 until piece measures 10½".

Bind off in pattern stitch.

Crocheting the Granny Square

STARTER ROUND Using CC and crochet hook, ch 6, join with slip stitch to form a ring, ch 1.

ROUND 1 Work 12 sc into the ring, slip stitch to first sc. Draw yarn through to fasten off, then break yarn.

ROUND 2 Attach MC to any sc of Round 1. Ch 6 (counts as 1 tr and 2 ch), skip 1 sc, (1 tr into next stitch, ch 2) 11 times, slip stitch to fourth chain of ch-6. Draw yarn through to fasten off, then break yarn.

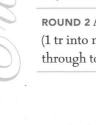

ROUND 3 Attach CC to any ch-2 space. Ch 3 (counts as 1 dc), 2 dc, * (1 sc into next space, ch 2) twice, (3 dc, ch 2, 3 dc) into next space, ch 2; repeat from * two more times, ending (1 sc into next space, ch 2) twice, 3 dc into next space, ch 2, slip stitch to third chain of ch-3. Draw yarn through to fasten off, then break yarn.

ROUND 4 Attach MC to ch-2 space at corner. Ch 3 (counts as 1 dc), 2 dc, * (1 sc into next space, ch 2) three times, (3 dc, ch 2, 3 dc) into corner space, ch 2; repeat from * two more times, ending (sc into next space, ch 2) three times, 3 dc into corner space, ch 2, slip stitch to third chain of ch-3. Draw the yarn through to fasten off, then break yarn.

ROUND 5 Attach CC to any stitch. Ch 1, work around edge in sc, making 2 sc in each space, 1 sc in each stitch, and 3 sc in each corner space; slip stitch to first sc. Draw yarn through to fasten off, then break yarn.

Finish

① Fold purse in half, leaving a ¼" (0.6 cm) extension along top back edge. Using MC and yarn needle, sew sides closed.

② Sew Granny Square to top back edge to form a flap that folds forward onto front of purse.

③ Sew two magnetic snap halves to front of purse and wrong side of flap.

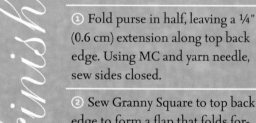

Accessorize!

Flower Garden Felted Bag

Is it a "knit" bag or a "knitting" bag? Either way it's a bag full of fun. A perfect first felting project because it's small, and, more important, it doesn't have to fit you! So if you shrink it a little too much, just stretch it out; and if it's too big, you can always shrink it some more. Fanciful crochet flowers stand at attention across the front of the bag just waiting to make any day a garden party.

Finished Measurements
14" × 9" (35 cm × 22.5 cm), plus handle

Yarn
Cascade 220, 100% Peruvian highland wool, 3.5 oz (100 g)/220 yds (201 m)
MC = 1 skein #9420 (dark teal)
CA = 1 skein #7809 (lilac)
CB = 1 skein #8888 (purple)
CC = 1 skein #8908 (turquoise)
CD = 1 skein #8910 (chartreuse)

Tools
Knit US #9 (5.5 mm) straight needles, or size you need to obtain correct gauge
Crochet Size G/6 (4.25 mm) crochet hook, or size you need to obtain correct gauge

Gauge
Knit 18 sts and 21 rows = 4" × 4" (10 cm × 10 cm) in Stockinette Stitch, *before felting*
Crochet 1 flower = 3" (7.5 cm) across

Other Supplies
Large-eye yarn needle
Crewel needle
Wooden purse handles (2), 10" × 5¼" (25 cm × 13 cm), or handles with a 7¾"/19 cm opening
Sewing thread to match MC
Hand-sewing needle

Abbreviations
CA = contrasting color A
CB = contrasting color B
CC = contrasting color C
CD = contrasting color D
ch = chain (verb)
ch- = chained loop or chained space
dtr = double treble crochet
hdc = half double crochet
K2tog = knit 2 together
MC = main color
sc = single crochet
ssk = slip, slip, knit these 2 stitches together
St st = stockinette stitch
tr = treble crochet
yo = yarn over

Pattern Stitches

Flower Pattern Stitch

SET UP Ch 4, join with slip stitch to first chain to form ring, ch 1.

NOTE *For the dtr (double treble crochet) in Round 4 below, wrap the yarn around the hook three times.*

ROUND 1 Work 10 hdc into ring.

ROUND 2 Ch 2 (counts as hdc), hdc into same space, work 2 hdc into each hdc around. *You now have* 20 hdc.

ROUND 3 Inserting hook into front loop of stitches only, * ch 3, 1 tr into base of ch-3, 2 tr into each of next 2 stitches, (1 tr, ch 3, slip stitch) into next hdc, slip stitch into next hdc; repeat from * four more times. Draw yarn through last stitch to fasten off, then break yarn. *You now have* 5 small petals.

ROUND 4 Join yarn into back loop of any center tr of one petal. Inserting hook into back loop of stitches only, * ch 3, 1 dtr into same place, 2 dtr into each of next 2 sts, (1 dtr, ch 3, slip stitch) into next hdc, slip stitch into next hdc; repeat from * four more times. Draw yarn through last stitch to fasten off, then break yarn. *You now have* 5 large petals.

ROUND 5 Join yarn into any Round-1 hdc on front of work, (ch 3, sc) into each stitch in round. End with slip stitch into base of ch-3. Draw yarn through last stitch to fasten off, and break yarn. *You now have* center ruffle.

Bobble Pattern Stitch

Using CD, ch 4. * Yo, insert hook into fourth chain from hook and draw up a loop, yo, draw through 2 loops on hook; repeat from * three more times. Yo and pull yarn through all 5 loops on hook. Pull yarn through last loop to fasten off, then, leaving a long tail, break yarn. Make 5.

Knitting the Bag (make 2)

SET UP Using MC and straight needles, cast on 54 stitches.

NOTE To "increase 1" in this pattern, knit into the front and into back of the next stitch.

Shaping the Bottom

ROW 1 (RIGHT SIDE) Knit to end of row.

ROW 2 (WRONG SIDE) Purl to end of row.

ROW 3 K1, increase 1, knit to last 2 stitches, increase 1, K1. You now have 56 sts.

ROW 4 Purl to end of row.

ROWS 5–14 Repeat Rows 3 and 4. You now have 66 sts.

ROWS 15–48 Work even in St st, ending with a purl row.

Shaping the Top

ROW 1 K1, ssk, knit to last 3 stitches, K2tog, K1. You now have 64 sts.

ROW 2 Purl to end of row.

ROW 3 Knit to end of row.

ROW 4 Purl to end of row.

ROWS 5–28 Repeat rows 1–4. You now have 52 sts.

ROWS 29–66 Work even in stockinette stitch.

ROW 67 Bind off 6 stitches in knit, knit to end of row. You now have 46 sts.

ROW 68 Bind off 6 stitches in purl, purl to end of row. You now have 40 sts.

ROWS 69–78 Work even in stockinette stitch. Bind off.

Make another identical piece.

Crocheting the Flowers

NOTE Referring to Flower Pattern Stitch, follow the color notes and additional instructions below to make Flowers 1–5. The smaller flowers (1, 4, and 5) omit Round 4.

Flower 1

Using CA, work Rounds 1–3. (Omit Round 4.)

Using CB, work Round 5.

Using CD, work bobble for for center.

Flower 2

Using CC, work Rounds 1–4.

Using CB, work Round 5.

Using CD, work bobble for center.

Flower 3

Using CB, work Rounds 1–4.

Using CA, work Round 5. Work the same ruffle around the edge of the larger petals.

Using CD, work bobble for center.

Flower 4

Using CB, work Rounds 1–3. (Omit Round 4.)

Using CB, work Round 5. Work the same ruffle around the outer edge of Round 3.

Using CD, work bobble for center.

Flower 5

Using CC, work Rounds 1–3. (Omit Round 4.)

Using CC, work Round 5. Work the same ruffle around the outer edge of Round 3.

Using CD, work bobble for center.

TEST FELT FOR SUCCESS Before washing your finished knitted bag, test-felt a swatch, 4" (10 cm) square, so that you can record the temperature and time it takes to get the look you want. Here's how: Fill your washing machine with hot water (about 100°–110°F/40°–45°C) on a small-load setting. Add ⅛ cup of baking soda and ¼–½ cup detergent. Add a small towel (for abrasion and balanced agitation) and your swatch. Use a 10- to 12-minute wash cycle, including cold rinse and spin. Take the swatch out and check the size: you want it to shrink to about 3½" (8.75 cm) square; the stitch definition should be nearly invisible. Repeat the process, if necessary, checking every few minutes until the size is right. Record the settings and cycle lengths, and use them when you felt the bag.

Finish

① Using MC and yarn needle, sew together Front and Back along sides and bottom, leaving side seams open 2" (5 cm) from top.

② Felt the purse using the settings and timing you used for your swatch (see Test Felt for Success, above).

③ Referring to the drawing opposite, pin flowers to bag front and stitch them securely in place.

④ Using crewel needle and CD, and referring to drawing, embroider five stems in chain stitch beneath the flowers.

⑤ Insert each handle extension at the top of the bag through a handle slot. Use matching thread and needle to sew each extension securely to the inside of the bag.

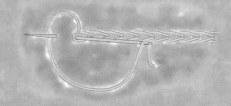

chain stitch

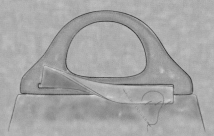

Back-to-School Backpack

Pack up your pencils and books! It's off to school with your one-of-a-kind backpack. The body of the bag is knit in a super-sturdy slip stitch, so it can stand up to the challenge of the little owner's stash. Crochet the granny-square flap for a bit of fun and whimsy. Worked in a denim-look suede yarn, it will surely inspire your little genius to make the grade.

Finished Measurements
10" (25 cm) square

Yarn
Suede by Berroco, 100% nylon,
   1¾ oz (50 g)/120 yds (111 m)
MC = 4 balls #3768 Indigo
CC = 1 ball #3727 (white)

Tools
Knit US #9 (5.5 mm) straight needles, or
   size you need to obtain correct gauge
Crochet Size G/6 (4.25 mm) crochet hook,
   or size you need to obtain correct gauge

Gauge
Knit 22 sts and 36 rows = 4" × 4"
   (10 cm × 10 cm) in Slip Stitch
   Pattern Stitch
Crochet 1 square = 5" × 5"
   (12.5 cm × 12.5 cm)

Other Supplies
Large-eye yarn needle
Magnetic snap

Abbreviations
CC = contrasting color
ch = chain (verb)
ch- = chained loop or chained space
dc = double crochet
MC = main color
sc = single crochet
tr = treble crochet

Pattern Stitches

Slip Stitch Pattern Stitch

ROW 1 (RIGHT SIDE) * K1, move yarn to front, slip 1 purlwise, move yarn to back; repeat from * to end of row.

ROW 2 * P1, move yarn to back, slip 1 purlwise, move yarn to front; repeat from * to end of row.

Knitting the Backpack

SET UP Using MC and straight needles, cast on 56 sts.

ROW 1 Work Row 1 of Slip Stitch Pattern Stitch.

ROW 2 Work Row 2 of Slip Stitch Pattern Stitch.

Repeat Rows 1 and 2 until piece measures 20½" (51 cm).

Bind off in pattern stitch.

Crocheting the Granny Square (make 4)

STARTER ROUND Using CC and crochet hook, ch 6, join with slip stitch to form a ring, ch 1.

ROUND 1 Work 12 sc into the ring, slip stitch to first sc. Draw yarn through to fasten off, then break yarn.

ROUND 2 Attach MC to any sc of Round 1. Ch 6 (counts as 1 tr and 2 ch), skip 1 sc, (1 tr into next stitch, ch 2) 11 times, slip stitch to fourth chain of ch-6. Draw yarn through to fasten off, then break yarn.

ROUND 3 Attach CC to any ch-2 space. Ch 3 (counts as 1 dc), 2 dc, * (1 sc into next space, ch 2) twice, (3 dc, ch 2, 3 dc) into next space, ch 2; repeat from * two more times, ending (1 sc into next space, ch 2) twice, 3 dc into next space, ch 2, slip stitch to third chain of ch-3. Draw yarn through to fasten off, then break yarn.

ROUND 4 Attach MC to ch-2 space at corner. Ch 3 (counts as 1 dc), 2 dc, * (1 sc into next space, ch 2) three times, (3 dc, ch 2, 3 dc) into corner space, ch 2; repeat from * two more times, ending (sc into next space, ch 2) three times, 3 dc into corner space, ch 2, slip stitch to third chain of ch-3. Draw the yarn through to fasten off, then break yarn.

ROUND 5 Attach CC to any stitch. Ch 1, work around edge in sc, making 2 sc in each space, 1 sc in each stitch, and 3 sc in each corner space; slip stitch to first sc. Draw yarn through to fasten off, then break yarn.

Crocheting the Strap

SET UP Using MC and crochet hook, work a chain 20" (50 cm) long.

ROW 1 Sc in second chain from hook and in each one across, ch 1, turn.

ROWS 2–4 Repeat Row 1. Draw yarn through to fasten off, then break yarn.

① Using CC and yarn needle, sew Granny Squares edge to edge in pairs. Sew the pairs together to make a 2 × 2 grid.

② Fold backpack in half with wrong sides facing, leaving a ¼" (.6 cm) extension along top back edge. Using MC and yarn needle, sew sides closed.

③ Sew Granny Square piece to top back edge of backpack to form a flap that folds forward over front.

④ Firmly stitch the strap to the back of the pack at the top corners and center bottom as shown in the illustration.

⑤ Attach pom pom to center bottom of flap, if desired.

Step 3

Step 4

Granny-Square Dog Sweater with Leash

Keeping Fido toasty and tasteful is no problem with this fashionable granny sweater. It's worked in jewel tones in a buttery-soft suede yarn that is both elegant and sturdy. The front is knit in a simple rib stitch so that it easily slips over the head; the back is made up of simple, colorful granny squares. So easy and quick you can make one for each of your four-legged friends!

Sizes and Finished Measurements
Small/Medium (4–5 pounds/1.8–2.3 k)
11½"/28.8 cm long (including collar, turned down); 16"/40 cm circumference
Medium/Large (10–15 pounds/4.5–6.8 k)
16"/40 cm long (including collar, turned down); 19"/47.5 cm circumference

Yarn
Berroco Suede, 100% nylon, 1.75 oz. (50 g)/120 yds (111 m) balls
MC = 1 ball #3719 Texas Rose
CA = 1 ball #3715 Tonto
CB = 1 ball #3745 Calamity Jane

Tools
Knit US #8 (5 mm) straight needles, or size you need to obtain correct gauge
Crochet Size H/8 (5 mm) crochet hook, or size you need to obtain correct gauge

Gauge
Knit 19 stitches and 28 rows = 4" × 4" (10 cm × 10 cm) in K1, P1 Rib Stitch
Crochet Small/Medium granny square = 3½" (8.8 cm); Medium/Large granny square = 4¼" (10.6 cm)

Other Supplies
2 stitch holders
Large-eye yarn needle

Abbreviations
CA = contrasting color A
CB = contrasting color B
ch = chain (verb)
ch- = chained loop or chained space
dc = double crochet
K2tog = knit 2 together
MC = main color
P2tog = purl 2 together
sc = single crochet

Pattern Stitches

Granny Square Pattern Stitch

NOTE *Work squares from right side: do not turn at ends of rounds. Always count the ch-3 (chain 3) at the beginning of a round as the first double crochet.*

SET UP Using CA, ch 4; join chain with a slip stitch to first chain to form a ring.

ROUND 1 (RIGHT SIDE) Ch 3 (counts as first dc in ring), 2 dc into ring, ch 2 (for corner space), * 3 dc into ring, ch 2; repeat from * twice more, 2 dc, slip stitch into top of ch-3 to close. Draw yarn through last stitch to fasten off, then break yarn. *You now have* 4 CA groups.

ROUND 2 Attach MC in any corner ch-2 space. (Ch 3, 2 dc, ch 2, 3 dc) in same space, * ch 2, (3 dc, ch 2, 3 dc) in next corner space; repeat from * twice more, ch 2, slip stitch into top of ch-3 to close. Draw yarn through last stitch to fasten off, then break yarn. *You now have* 8 MC groups.

ROUND 3 Attach CB in any corner ch-2 space. Ch 3, (2 dc, ch 2, 3 dc) in same space, ch 1, * 3 dc in next ch-2 space, ch 1, (3 dc, ch 2, 3 dc) in next ch-2 corner space, ch 1; repeat from * twice more, 3 dc in next ch-2 space, ch 1. Slip stitch into top of ch-3 to close. Draw yarn through last stitch to fasten off, then break yarn. *You now have* 12 CB groups.

ROUND 4 (MEDIUM/LARGE ONLY) Attach CA in any corner ch-2 space. (Ch 3, 2 dc, ch 2, 3 dc) in same space, ch 1, * (3 dc in next ch-1 space, ch 1) twice, (3 dc, ch 2, 3 dc) in next corner space, ch 1; repeat from * twice more, (3 dc in next ch-1 space, ch 1) twice, slip stitch into top of ch-3 to close. Draw yarn through last stitch to fasten off, then break yarn. *You now have* 16 CA groups.

Crocheting the Back

① Following the Granny Square Pattern Stitch, crochet six granny squares.

② Arrange the granny squares in two rows of three squares each. With two squares adjoining, attach CB (for Small/Medium) or MC (for Medium/Large) in corner ch-2 space of first square.

③ Insert crochet hook from right side into corner ch-2 space of first square, pull up a loop, sc in same space, ch 1, insert hook from right side into corresponding ch-2 space of second square and work slip stitch; * ch 1, skip 1 stitch of first square, slip stitch from right side into next stitch, ch 1, skip 1 stitch of second square, slip stitch from right side into next stitch; repeat from * to end of seam. Break off yarn. Repeat to join three squares. Make another row with the remaining three squares.

④ Crochet the rows together in the same manner.

⑤ Attach CA (for Small/Medium) or MC (for Medium/Large) at X (see illustration below). 1 sc (skip 1 stitch, 1 sc) to Y (top of Back). Continue to work sc in every stitch from Y to starting point. Set aside Back.

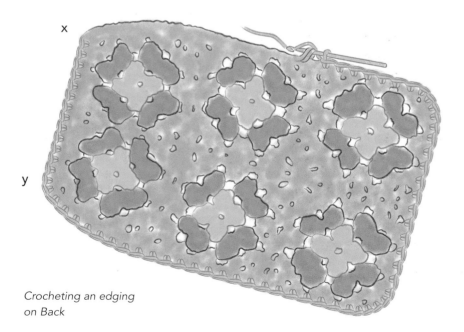

*Crocheting an edging
on Back*

Knitting the Front

	[SM/MD]	[MD/LG]

NOTE Except for the stripes at the edge of the turtleneck collar, use MC for the entire body of the sweater. The body is worked in a K1, P1 rib; the legs are worked in Garter Stitch.

	[SM/MD]	[MD/LG]
SET UP Using MC and straight needles, cast on	37 sts	45 sts
ROW 1 (RIGHT SIDE) * K1, P1; repeat from * to end of row, ending K1.		
ROW 2 * P1, K1; repeat from * to end of row, ending P1.		
NEXT ROWS REPEAT ROWS 1 AND 2	1 more time	4 more times

Section 1

	[SM/MD]	[MD/LG]
SET UP (K1, P1) to end of row	3 times	4 times
For right leg, cast on	6 sts	8 sts
Place remaining stitches on a stitch holder. In the following section, you will be working only the right side and leg stitches. You now have	12 sts	16 sts
ROW 1 Knit the leg stitches, then P1, K1 to end of row.		
ROW 2 Maintain the K1, P1 ribbing as established, then knit the leg stitches.	(6 sts)	(8 sts)
NEXT ROWS Ending with a right-side row, repeat Rows 1 and 2 until length from beginning of leg (cast-on stitches) measures	2" (5 cm)	3½" (8.8 cm)
NEXT ROW At the beginning of the next row, bind off the leg stitches.	(6 sts)	(8 sts)
FINISH Place remaining stitches on a stitch holder.		

Section 2

	[SM/MD]	[MD/LG]
SET UP Remove from stitch holder and place on a needle the next	25 sts	29 sts
With picked-up stitches on the left-hand needle, for right leg, cast on	6 sts	8 sts

	[SM/MD]		[MD/LG]
Knit the cast-on stitches, then work in established K1, P1 ribbing. For left leg, cast on	6 sts	•	8 sts
You now have	37 sts	•	45 sts
NOTE The number of stitches remaining on the stitch holder is	6	•	8
ROW 1 Knit the leg stitches, work the established ribbing, knit the remaining	6 sts	•	8 sts
NEXT ROWS Repeat Row 1 until length from beginning of leg (cast-on stitches) measures	2" (5 cm)	•	3½" (8.8 cm)
End with a wrong-side row.			
NEXT ROWS At the beginning of the next two rows, bind off the leg stitches, maintaining the pattern as established.			
FINISH Place on a stitch holder the remaining	35 sts	•	45 sts

Section 3

	[SM/MD]		[MD/LG]
SET UP Remove from stitch holder and place on a needle the remaining original	6 sts	•	8 sts
With picked-up stitches on the left-hand needle, for left leg, cast on	6 sts	•	8 sts
ROW 1 Knit the leg stitches, then K1, P1 to end of row.			
ROW 2 K1, P1 in established ribbing, then end	K6 sts	•	K8 sts
NEXT ROWS Repeat Rows 1 and 2 until length from beginning of leg (cast-on stitches) measures	2" (5 cm)	•	3½" (8.8 cm)
End with a wrong-side row.			
FINISH At the beginning of the next row, bind off the leg stitches. Place remaining stitches on a stitch holder.			
Slip all the stitches from the holders to the same needle, beginning with right-side stitches, then center-front stitches, and left-side stitches. You now have	37 sts	•	45 sts

KNITTING THE FRONT (continued)	[SM/MD]		[MD/LG]
Work established ribbing for	½" (1.25 cm)	•	¾" (1.9 cm)
End with a wrong-side row.			
SET UP With right side of crocheted Back facing and with the knitted front stitches on the right-hand needle (right side just completed), pick up and knit	26 sts	•	28 sts
You now have	63 sts	•	73 sts
ROW 1 * K1, P1; repeat from * to end of row, ending K1.			
ROW 2 * K8, P2tog, K2tog; repeat from *, ending K3. You now have	51 sts	•	61 sts
NEXT ROWS Work in established ribbing pattern until piece measures 2" (5 cm) from picked-up stitches.			
Change yarn to CB and work two rows in ribbing pattern.			
Change yarn to MC and work two rows in ribbing pattern.			
Change yarn to CA, and work one row in ribbing pattern.			
Using CA, bind off in ribbing.			

Finish

① Using yarn needle and matching yarn, sew the turtleneck collar side seam, taking care to adjust the right and wrong sides so that the seam is hidden when the turtleneck is turned down.

② With right sides together, sew Front to Back at side edges.

③ With right sides together, sew the two side edges of each leg opening to create a small sleeve.

④ Using desired-color yarn for back-leg strap, ch 18. Turn, sc in each chain across. Draw yarn through last stitch to fasten off, then break yarn. Make a second strap.

⑤ Place straps diagonally across lower corners on wrong side of Back. Fasten securely to edges.

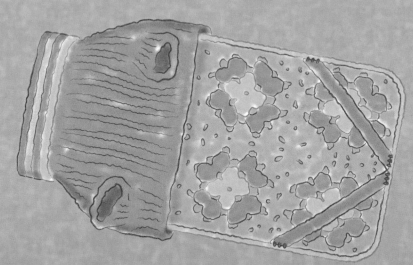

Attaching the straps on the lower inside of Back

Dog Leash

As a complement to your pooch's wardrobe, work up this sturdy, knit-from-nylon item for a truly new "leash" on life.

Finished Measurements
½" × 40" (1.25 cm × 1 m),
   plus swivel clip

Yarn
Coats & Clark Crochet Nylon, 100% nylon,
   1.75 oz (50 g)/150 yds (137 m)
1 tube #49 Country Blue

Tools
Knit Two US #7 (4.5 mm) double-point
   needles, or size you need to obtain
   correct gauge
Crochet Size F/5 (4 mm) crochet hook, or
   size you need to obtain correct gauge

Gauge
Knit 23 sts = 4" (10 cm)
   in knitted cord
Crochet 14 sc = 4" (10 cm)

Other Supplies
Large-eye yarn needle
Leash swivel clip

Abbreviations
ch = chain (verb)
K2tog = knit 2 together
sc = single crochet

Knitting the Leash

SET UP Using two double-point needles, cast on 5 stitches.

ROUND 1 Knit across the row. Do not turn.

ROUND 2 Slide the stitches back to the other end of the needle. Firmly drawing the yarn behind the stitches on the needle, knit all 5 stitches on the needle.

NEXT ROUNDS Repeat Round 2 until knitted cord measures 32" (80 cm).

Handle

ROW 1 K1, K2tog, K2.

NEXT ROWS Continue knitting in the round as above until knitted cord measures 40" (1 m).

FINISH Bind off all stitches.

Turn down 8" (20 cm) of cord to form handle. Using yarn needle and matching yarn, sew end in place.

Crocheting the Trim

① Insert crochet hook into side edge of handle and attach yarn. * Ch 3, skip 2 stitches, 1 sc into next stitch; repeat from * until you reach starting point, slip stitch to join. Draw yarn through last stitch to fasten, then break yarn.

② Repeat crochet trim around other side edge of handle.

Attaching Swivel Clip

Slip opposite end of leash through swivel end of dog leash clip and fold back ¾" (1.9 cm) (see photo on facing page). Using yarn needle and yarn, sew securely in place.

CHAPTER 2
Sassy Sweaters!

Simple Cardigan Touched with Crochet

This sweet little cardigan makes you want to sing "isn't it romantic," or maybe just dance around the room. On the other hand, it's just as at home with a pair of jeans and high tops. Any way you pair it, this basic knit sweater is sure to be the one piece you grab over and over again. The cotton yarn knit in simple stockinette stitch makes it lightweight and very versatile, and the crochet edging adds just the right finishing touch.

Sizes and Finished Chest Measurements
Small 34" (85 cm)
Medium 36" (90 cm)
Large 40" (1 m)

Yarn
Tahki Cotton Classic, 100% cotton,
  1.75 oz (50 g)/108 yds (99 m)
5 (6, 7) skeins #3451 Light Pink

Tools
Knit US #6 (4 mm) straight needles, or size
  you need to obtain correct gauge
Crochet Size G/6 (4.25 mm) crochet hook,
  or size you need to obtain correct gauge

Gauge
Knit 20 sts and 24 rows = 4" × 4"
  (10 cm × 10 cm) in stockinette stitch
Crochet 16 sc and 20 rows = 4" × 4"
  (10 cm × 10 cm) in sc

Other Supplies
Large-eye yarn needle

Abbreviations
ch = chain (verb)
ch- = chained loop or chained space
dc = double crochet
K2tog = knit 2 together
sc = single crochet
ssk = slip, slip, knit these 2 stitches
  together
St st = stockinette stitch

Knitting the Cardigan

	[S]	[M]	[L]

NOTE To "increase 1" means to knit into the front and the back of the next stitch.

Back

	[S]		[M]		[L]
SET UP Using straight needles, cast on	84 sts	•	90 sts	•	98 sts
STARTER ROW Knit to end of row.					
ROW 1 (WRONG SIDE) Purl to end of row.					
ROW 2 Knit to end of row.					
NEXT ROWS Repeat Rows 1 and 2, working even in St st, until piece measures	7" (17.5 cm)	•	7½" (18.75 cm)	•	8" (20 cm)
NEXT 2 ROWS Bind off 5 stitches at beginning of each row, then work even to end of row. You now have	74 sts	•	80 sts	•	88 sts
NEXT ROWS Work even in St st until piece measures	15" (37.5 cm)	•	16" (40 cm)	•	17" (42.5 cm)

Bind off all stitches.

Left Front

	[S]		[M]		[L]
SET UP Using straight needles, cast on	8 sts	•	11 sts	•	14 sts
STARTER ROW Knit to end of row.					
ROW 1 (WRONG SIDE) Cast on 7 stitches. Purl to end of row. You now have	15 sts	•	18 sts	•	21 sts
ROW 2 Knit	6 sts	•	7 sts	•	8 sts
then increase 1, knit to end. You now have	16 sts	•	19 sts	•	22 sts
ROW 3 Cast on 6 stitches. Purl to end of row. You now have	22 sts	•	25 sts	•	28 sts
ROW 4 Knit to end of row.					
ROW 5 Cast on 5 stitches. Purl to end of row. You now have	27 sts	•	30 sts	•	33 sts

	[S]		[M]		[L]
ROW 6 Repeat Row 2. You now have	28 sts	•	31 sts	•	34 sts
ROW 7 Cast on 4 stitches. Purl to end of row. You now have	32 sts	•	35 sts	•	38 sts
ROW 8 Knit to end of row.					
ROW 9 Cast on 3 stitches. Purl to end of row. You now have	35 sts	•	38 sts	•	41 sts
ROW 10 Repeat Row 2. You now have	36 sts	•	39 sts	•	42 sts
ROW 11 Cast on 2 stitches. Purl to end of row. You now have	38 sts	•	41 sts	•	44 sts
ROW 12 Knit to end of row.					
ROW 13 Cast on 1 stitch. Purl to end of row. You now have	39 sts	•	42 sts	•	45 sts
ROW 14 Repeat Row 2. You now have	40 sts	•	43 sts	•	46 sts
ROW 15 Repeat Row 13. You now have	41 sts	•	44 sts	•	47 sts
ROW 16 Knit to end of row.					
ROW 17 Purl to end of row.					

Neck Shaping

	[S]		[M]		[L]
ROW 1 Knit	6 sts	•	7 sts	•	8 sts
then increase 1, knit to last 4 stitches, end K2tog, K2. You now have	41 sts	•	44 sts	•	47 sts
ROW 2 Purl to end of row.					
ROW 3 Knit to end of row.					
ROW 4 Purl to end of row.					
ROW 5 Repeat Row 1. You now have	41 sts	•	44 sts	•	47 sts
ROW 6 Purl to end of row.					
ROW 7 Knit to end of row.					
ROW 8 Purl to end of row.					

Knit

KNITTING THE CARDIGAN (continued)

	[S]	[M]	[L]
ROW 9 Knit to last 4 stitches, end K2tog, K2. You now have	40 sts	43 sts	46 sts
NEXT ROWS Repeat Rows 6–9 until piece measures	7" (17.5 cm)	7½" (18.75 cm)	8" (20 cm)

Armhole Shaping

	[S]	[M]	[L]
SET UP (RIGHT SIDE) Bind off 5 stitches, work even for rest of row.			
NEXT ROWS Continue as established, decreasing 1 stitch (by K2tog) at neck edge every fourth row as before until piece measures	15" (37.5 cm)	16" (40 cm)	17" (42.5 cm)
Bind off all stitches.			

Right Front

	[S]	[M]	[L]
SET UP Using straight needles, cast on	8 sts	11 sts	14 sts
STARTER ROW Knit to end of row.			
ROW 1 (WRONG SIDE) Purl to end of row, cast on 7 stitches. You now have	15 sts	18 sts	21 sts
ROW 2 Knit 7 stitches, increase 1, knit to end of row. You now have	16 sts	19 sts	22 sts
ROW 3 Purl to end of row, cast on 6 stitches. You now have	22 sts	25 sts	28 sts
ROW 4 Knit to end of row.			
ROW 5 Purl to end of row, cast on 5 stitches. You now have	27 sts	30 sts	33 sts
ROW 6 Knit 19 stitches, increase 1, knit to end of row. You now have	28 sts	31 sts	34 sts
ROW 7 Purl to end of row, cast on 4 stitches. You now have	32 sts	35 sts	38 sts

KNITTING THE CARDIGAN (continued)	[S]		[M]		[L]
ROW 8 Knit to end of row.					
ROW 9 Purl to end of row, cast on 3 stitches. You now have	35 sts	•	38 sts	•	41 sts
ROW 10 Knit 27 stitches, increase 1, knit to end of row. You now have	36 sts	•	39 sts	•	42 sts
ROW 11 Purl to end of row, cast on 2 stitches. You now have	38 sts	•	41 sts	•	44 sts
ROW 12 Knit to end of row.					
ROW 13 Purl to end of row, cast on 1 stitch. You now have	39 sts	•	42 sts	•	45 sts
ROW 14 Knit 31 stitches, increase 1, knit to end of row. You now have	40 sts	•	43 sts	•	46 sts
ROW 15 Repeat Row 13. You now have	41 sts	•	44 sts	•	47 sts
ROW 16 Knit to end of row.					
ROW 17 Purl to end of row.					

Neck Shaping

	[S]		[M]		[L]
ROW 1 K2, ssk, knit	34 sts	•	36 sts	•	38 sts
then increase 1, knit	6 sts	•	7 sts	•	8 sts
You now have	41 sts	•	44 sts	•	47 sts
ROW 2 Purl to end of row.					
ROW 3 Knit to end of row.					
ROW 4 Purl to end of row.					
ROW 5 Repeat Row 1. You now have	41 sts	•	44 sts	•	47 sts
ROW 6 Purl to end of row.					
ROW 7 Knit to end of row.					
ROW 8 Purl to end of row.					

Knit

KNITTING THE CARDIGAN (continued)

	[S]		[M]		[L]
ROW 9 K2, ssk, knit to end of row. You now have	40 sts	•	43 sts	•	46 sts
NEXT ROWS Repeat Rows 6–9 until piece measures	7" (17.5 cm)	•	7½" (18.75 cm)	•	8" (20 cm)

Underarm Shaping

	[S]		[M]		[L]
NEXT ROW (RIGHT SIDE) Work even, bind off last 5 stitches.					
NEXT ROWS Continue as established, decreasing 1 stitch (by ssk) at neck edge every fourth row as before, until piece measures	15" (37.5 cm)	•	16" (40 cm)	•	17" (42.5 cm)

Bind off all stitches.

Sleeve

	[S]		[M]		[L]
SET UP Using straight needles, cast on	60 sts	•	64 sts	•	66 sts
ROW 1 (WRONG SIDE) * K1, P1; repeat from * to end of row.					
ROW 2 * P1, K1; repeat from * to end of row.					
ROWS 3–8 Repeat Rows 1 and 2 for ribbing.					
ROW 9 Purl to end of row.					
ROW 10 K1, increase 1, knit to last stitch, increase 1, K1. You now have	62 sts	•	66 sts	•	68 sts
ROW 11 Purl to end of row.					
ROW 12 Knit to end of row.					
NEXT ROWS Repeat Rows 1–4	12 times	•	13 times	•	14 times
You now have	86 sts	•	92 sts	•	96 sts
Work even in St st until piece measures	10" (25 cm)	•	11" (27.5 cm)	•	12" (30 cm)

Bind off all stitches.

Using yarn needle, sew shoulder and side seams. Sew each sleeve seam, leaving 1" (2.5 cm) open at underarm. Set sleeves into body.

Setting in the sleeve

then Crochet

Crocheting the Edging

SET UP Using crochet hook, attach yarn to left shoulder seam at the neck edge.

NOTE The stitch total in Starter Round must be evenly divisible by 4.

STARTER ROUND 1 sc in every other row down left neck edge, * (1 sc in 1 stitch) twice, skip 1 stitch; repeat from * across bottom edge. 1 sc in every other row up right neck edge. * (Make 1 sc in 1 stitch) twice, skip 1 stitch; repeat from * across back neck edge. End so total sc stitch count is evenly divisible by 4. Ch 3, turn.

ROUND 1 Skip 1 sc, * make 1 sc in next sc, ch 3, skip 1 sc, make 1 sc in next sc, ch 1, skip 1 sc; repeat from * around. Join with slip stitch to second ch of ch-3. Turn.

ROUND 2 * 1 sc in ch-1 sp, (1 dc, ch 2, 1 dc, ch 2, 1 dc) in ch-3 sp; repeat from * around, join with slip stitch to first sc. Draw yarn through last stitch to fasten off, then break yarn.

Tweed-and-Flowers Cardigan

Rich tweedy yarn creates a warm and inviting little cardi that's a perfect top layer to any outfit. Worked in a simple stockinette stitch (knit 1 row, purl 1 row), this sweater works up fast so you can indulge your corsage fantasy. The cascading crochet flowers and the delicate picot edging make a perfect counterpoint to the rugged tweed. Try out several flower variations to help you perfect your crocheting skills.

Sizes and Finished Chest Measurements
Small 34½" (86 cm)
Medium 36" (90 cm)
Large 38½" (96 cm)

Yarn
Rowan Yorkshire Tweed, 100% wool,
   1.75 oz (50 g)/123 yds (113 m)
MC = 8 (9, 10) balls #344 Scarlet
CA = 1 ball #350 Frolic
CB = 1 ball #343 Cheer
CC = 1 ball #342 Revel
CD = A few yards of any white worsted-
   weight yarn

Tools
Knit US #8 (5 mm) straight needles, or size
   you need to obtain correct gauge
Crochet Size H/8 (5 mm) crochet hook, or
   size you need to obtain correct gauge

Gauge
Knit 18 sts and 24 rows = 4" × 4"
   (10 cm × 10 cm) in Stockinette Stitch
Crochet 20 sts = 4" (10 cm) in sc

Other Supplies
Large-eye yarn needle

Abbreviations
CA = contrasting color A
CB = contrasting color B
CC = contrasting color C
CD = contrasting color D
ch = chain (verb)
ch- = chained loop or chained space
dtc = double treble crochet
hdc = half double crochet
K2tog = knit 2 together
MC = main color
P2tog = purl 2 together
sc = single crochet
ssk = slip, slip, knit these 2 stitches
   together
ssp = slip, slip, purl these 2 stitches
   together
St st = stockinette stitch
tr = treble crochet
yo = yarn over

Knitting the Cardigan

	[S]	[M]	[L]

NOTE To "increase 1," knit into the front and the back of the next stitch.

Back

	[S]		[M]		[L]
SET UP Using MC and straight needles, cast on	74 sts	•	76 sts	•	78 sts
ROW 1 Purl to end of row.					
ROW 2 Knit to end of row.					
ROW 3 Repeat Row 1.					
ROW 4 Repeat Row 2.					
ROW 5 Repeat Row 1.					
ROW 6 K1, increase 1, knit to last 2 stitches, increase 1, K1. You now have	76 sts	•	78 sts	•	80 sts
NEXT ROWS Repeat Rows 1–6	5 times	•	6 times	•	7 times
You now have	86 sts	•	90 sts	•	94 sts
Work even in St st until piece measures	7" (17.5 cm)	•	8" (20 cm)	•	9" (22.5 cm)
NEXT 2 ROWS Bind off 5 stitches; work even to end of row. You now have	76 sts	•	80 sts	•	84 sts
NEXT ROWS Work even until piece measures	15" (37.5 cm)	•	16" (40 cm)	•	17½" (43.75 cm)
Bind off all stitches.					

Right Front

	[S]		[M]		[L]
SET UP Using MC and straight needles, cast on	23 sts	•	24 sts	•	25 sts
ROW 1 Purl to end of row.					
ROW 2 K1, increase 1, knit to last 2 stitches, increase 1, K1. You now have	24 sts	•	25 sts	•	26 sts
ROW 3 Repeat Row 1.					

KNITTING THE CARDIGAN (continued)	[S]		[M]		[L]
ROW 4 K1, increase 1, knit to end of row. You now have	25 sts	•	26 sts	•	27 sts
ROW 5 Repeat Row 1.					
ROW 6 K1, increase 1, knit to last 2 stitches, increase 1, K1. You now have	27 sts	•	28 sts	•	29 sts
ROWS 7–24 Repeat Rows 1–6 three times. You now have	39 sts	•	40 sts	•	41 sts
ROWS 25, 27, AND 29 Purl to end of row.					
ROWS 26 AND 28 Knit to end of row.					
ROW 30 Knit to last 2 stitches, increase 1, K1. You now have	40 sts	•	41 sts	•	42 sts
NEXT ROWS Repeat Rows 25–30	once	•	twice	•	3 times
You now have	41 sts	•	42 sts	•	45 sts
Work even until piece measures	7" (17.5 cm)	•	8" (20 cm)	•	9" (22.5 cm)

Armhole Shaping

	[S]		[M]		[L]
ROW 1 (WRONG SIDE) Bind off 5 stitches; purl to end of row. You now have	36 sts	•	37 sts	•	40 sts
Work even in St st until piece measures	11" (27.5 cm)	•	12" (30 cm)	•	13" (32.5 cm)

Neck Shaping

	[S]		[M]		[L]
ROW 1 (RIGHT SIDE) Bind off 4 stitches; knit to end of row. You now have	32 sts	•	33 sts	•	36 sts
ROW 2 Purl to end of row.					
ROW 3 Bind off 2 stitches; knit to end of row. You now have	30 sts	•	31 sts	•	34 sts
ROW 4 Purl to last 3 stitches, P2tog, P1.					

Knit

	[S]		[M]		[L]
ROW 5 K1, ssk, knit to end of row.					
Repeat Rows 4 and 5 three times. *You now have*	22 sts	•	24 sts	•	26 sts
Work even in St st until piece measures	15" (37.5 cm)	•	16" (40 cm)	•	17½" (43.75 cm)
Bind off all stitches.					

Left Front

	[S]		[M]		[L]
SET UP Using MC and straight needles, cast on	23 sts	•	24 sts	•	25 sts
ROW 1 Purl to end of row.					
ROW 2 Knit to last 2 stitches, increase 1, K1. *You now have*	24 sts	•	25 sts	•	26 sts
ROW 3 Repeat Row 1.					
ROW 4 Knit to last 2 stitches, increase 1, K1. *You now have*	25 sts	•	26 sts	•	27 sts
ROW 5 Repeat Row 1.					
ROW 6 K1, increase 1, knit to last 2 stitches, increase 1, K1. *You now have*	27 sts	•	28 sts	•	29 sts
ROWS 7–24 Repeat Rows 1–6 three times. *You now have*	39 sts	•	40 sts	•	41 sts
ROWS 25, 27, AND 29 Purl to end of row.					
ROWS 26 AND 28 Knit to end of row.					
ROW 30 K1, increase 1, knit to end of row. *You now have*	40 sts	•	41 sts	•	42 sts
NEXT ROWS Repeat Rows 25–30	once	•	twice	•	3 times
You now have	41 sts	•	42 sts	•	45 sts

KNITTING THE CARDIGAN (continued)	[S]	[M]	[L]
Work even until piece measures	7" (17.5 cm)	8" (20 cm)	9" (22.5 cm)

Armhole Shaping

	[S]	[M]	[L]
ROW 1 (WRONG SIDE) Purl to end of row, bind off 5 stitches. You now have	36 sts	37 sts	40 sts
Work even in St st until piece measures	11" (27.5 cm)	12" (30 cm)	13" (32.5 cm)

Neck Shaping

	[S]	[M]	[L]
ROW 1 (RIGHT SIDE) Knit to end of row, bind off 4 stitches. You now have	32 sts	33 sts	36 sts
ROW 2 Purl to end of row.			
ROW 3 Knit to end of row, bind off 2 stitches. You now have	30 sts	31 sts	34 sts
ROW 4 P1, ssp, purl to end of row.			
ROW 5 Knit to last 3 stitches, K2tog, K1.			
Repeat Rows 4 and 5 three times. You now have	22 sts	24 sts	26 sts
Work even in St st until piece measures	15" (37.5 cm)	16" (40 cm)	17½" (43.75 cm)

Bind off all stitches.

Sleeves (make 2)

	[S]	[M]	[L]
SET UP Using MC and straight needles, cast on	36 sts	38 sts	40 sts
ROWS 1, 3, 7, AND 9 Purl to end of row.			
ROWS 2, 4, 6, AND 8 Knit to end of row.			

Knit

	[S]		[M]		[L]
ROW 5 P1, increase 1, purl to last 2 stitches, increase 1, P1. You now have	38 sts	•	40 sts	•	42 sts
ROW 10 K1, increase 1, knit to last 2 stitches, increase 1, K1. You now have	40 sts	•	42 sts	•	44 sts
NEXT ROWS Repeat Rows 1–10	8 times	•	7 times	•	8 times
then repeat Rows 1–5	(none)	•	one time	•	(none)
You now have	72 sts	•	72 sts	•	76 sts
Work even in St st until piece measures	16" (40 cm)	•	17" (42.5 cm)	•	18" (45 cm)

Bind off all stitches.

Crocheting the Flowers

Flower 1

SET UP With CA, chain 19.

ROW 1 Sc in second chain from hook, (ch 4, skip 1, sc in next chain) 4 times, (ch 3, skip 1, sc in next chain) 2 times, (ch 2, skip 1, sc in next chain) 3 times, turn.

ROW 2 (2 sc, 3 hdc, 2 sc) in first ch-2 space, (1 sc, 3 hdc, 1 sc) in next ch-2 space. Change to CC. (1 hdc, 3 dc, 1 hdc) in next ch-2 space, (1 hdc, 2 dc, 1 tr, 2 dc, 1 hdc) in each ch-3 space, (1 hdc, 2 dc, 3 tr, 2 dc, 1 hdc) in each chain of the ch-4 spaces.

Draw yarn through last stitch to fasten off, then break yarn, leaving a 6" (15 cm) tail to use to attach the flower to the sweater.

ROW 3 Join CA, and sc in each stitch of the last 4 CC petals. Draw yarn through last stitch to fasten off, then break yarn.

FINISHING At the smaller petal end, thread a yarn tail into a large-eye yarn needle, and sew a line of running stitches along the base chain. Pull on the yarn to roll up the petals, so that the smallest petals form the inner part of the flower.

Use the yarn tails to attach the flower to the sweater.

CROCHETING THE FLOWERS (continued)

Flower 2

SET UP With MC, chain 20.

ROW 1 Sc in second chain from hook, (ch 4, skip 1, 1 sc in next chain) 4 times, (ch 3, skip 1, 1 sc in next chain) 2 times, (ch 2, skip 1, 1 sc in next chain) 3 times. Turn.

ROW 2 (2 sc, 3 hdc, 2 sc) in first ch-2 space, (1 sc, 3 hdc, 1 sc) in next ch-2 space, (1 hdc, 3 dc, 1 hdc) in next ch-2 space, (1 hdc, 2 dc, 1 tr, 2 dc, 1 hdc) in each ch-3 space, (1 hdc, 2 dc, 3 tr, 2 dc, 1 hdc) in each chain of the ch-4 spaces.

Draw yarn through last stitch to fasten off, then break yarn, leaving a 6" (15 cm) tail to use to attach the flower to the sweater.

ROW 3 Join CC, and slip stitch in each stitch of Row 2.

FINISHING At the smaller petal end, thread a yarn tail into a large-eye yarn needle, and sew a line of running stitches along the base chain. Pull on the yarn to roll up the petals, so that the smallest petals form the inner part of the flower.

Use the yarn tails to attach the flower to the sweater.

Flower 3

SET UP With MC, chain 4, then join with a slip stitch to form a ring.

ROUND 1 * 1 hdc, ch 1; repeat from * five more times, then join with a slip stitch to the first hdc.

ROUND 2 * 1 sc in ch-1 space, ch 3; repeat from * to end of round, then join with a slip stitch to first sc.

ROUND 3 * 1 sc in sc, (1 hdc, 1 dc, 3 tr, 1 dc, 1 hdc) in ch-3 space; repeat from * to end of round, then join with a slip stitch to first sc.

Draw yarn through last stitch to fasten off, then break yarn.

Center Bobble

With CD, chain 3, yo, insert hook into third chain from hook and draw up a loop, * yo, draw through 2 loops on hook, yo, insert hook into same chain and draw up a loop; repeat from * two more times, yo, draw through 2 loops on hook, yo, draw through all 5 loops on hook. Draw yarn through last loop to fasten off; break yarn, leaving a 6" (15 cm) tail to attach bobble and flower to sweater.

CROCHETING THE FLOWERS (continued)

Flower 4

SET UP With CD, chain 4, then join with a slip stitch to form a ring.

ROUND 1 * 1 hdc, ch 1; repeat from * 5 more times, ending with a slip stitch to the first hdc. Change to CC.

ROUND 2 * 1 sc in ch-1 space, ch 3; repeat from * to end of round, then join with a slip stitch to the first sc.

ROUND 3 * 1 sc in sc, (1 hdc, 1 dc, 3 tr, 1 dc, 1 hdc) in ch-3 space; repeat from * to end of round, then join with a slip stitch to the first sc. Draw yarn through last stitch to fasten off, then break yarn.

ROUND 4 Join CD to back of center tr, 1 sc in same space, *ch 7, sc in back of next tr; repeat from * to end of round, then join with a slip stitch to the first sc.

ROUND 5 (1 hdc, 2 dc, 3 tr, 2 dc, 1 hdc) into each ch-7 space, then join with a slip stitch to the first hdc.

Draw yarn through last stitch to fasten off, then break yarn, leaving a 6" (15 cm) tail to use to attach the flower to the sweater.

Crocheting the Edging

Front, Neck, and Bottom

SET UP Using crochet hook and MC, attach yarn to right shoulder seam.

STARTER ROUND Work sc around entire edge as follows: On row edge, 1 sc in every other row; on stitch edge, * (1 sc in 1 stitch) twice, skip 1; repeat from * around all edges. Ch 1, turn.

PICOT TRIM * 1 sc, ch 4, 1 sc in fourth chain from hook, 1 sc in next sc; repeat from * around all edges, end slip stitch to first sc. Draw yarn through last stitch to fasten off, then break yarn.

Sleeve

Using crochet hook and MC, attach yarn to sleeve seam at wrist edge. Work Starter Round and Picot Trim around wrist edge. Repeat for second sleeve.

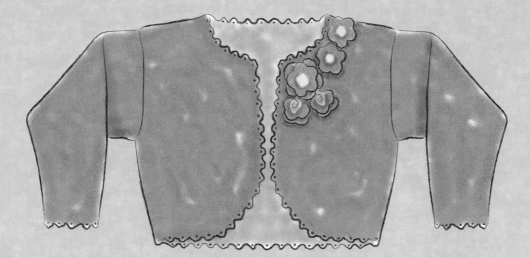

Finish

1. Using MC and yarn needle, sew shoulder and side seams.

2. Sew each sleeve seam, leaving 1" open at underarms. Set sleeves into body. (See illustration on page 89.)

3. Sew flowers in place as shown above.

Shaped Cardigan with Shell Sleeves

Shaped to flatter the figure, this one-button cardigan is a soft and sensual sweater that is sure to be a show-stopper. The interesting knit tuck stitch is a little challenging when combined with the shaping, but it's well worth the time. Crochet shell sleeves and edging provide the perfect finish.

Sizes and Finished Chest Measurements
Small/Medium 36" (90 cm)
Medium/Large 40½" (1 m)

Yarn
Rowan Classic Shades, Cashsoft DK, 57% extra-fine merino/33% microfibre/10% cashmere, 1¾ oz. (50 g)/142 yds (130 m)
6 (7) balls #506 Crush

Tools
Knit US #7 (4.5 mm) straight needles, or size you need to obtain correct gauge
Crochet Size G/6 (4.0, 4.25 mm) crochet hook, or size you need to obtain correct gauge

Gauge
Knit 20 sts and 32 rows = 4" × 4" (10 cm × 10 cm) in Knit Pattern Stitch
Crochet 16 sts and 8 rows = 4" (10 cm) in dc

Other Supplies
Large-eye yarn needle
One 1" (2.5 cm) button

Abbreviations
ch = chain (verb)
ch- = chained loop or chained space
dc = double crochet
hdc = half double crochet
K2tog = knit 2 together
P2tog = purl 2 together
sc = single crochet
ssk = slip, slip, knit these 2 stitches together
ssp = slip, slip, purl these 2 stitches together
tr = treble crochet

Pattern Stitches

Knit Pattern Stitch

ROWS 1, 3, AND 5 Knit to end of row.

ROWS 2 AND 4 Purl to end of row.

ROW 6 * K2tog; repeat from * to end of row.

ROW 7 K1, P1 in each stitch to end of row.

ROW 8 Purl to end of row.

Knitting the Cardigan

	[S]/[M]		[M]/[L]

Back

	[S]/[M]		[M]/[L]
NOTE To "increase 1", knit into the front and the back of the next stitch.			
SET UP Using straight needles, cast on	90 sts	•	102 sts
STARTER ROW (WRONG SIDE) Purl to end of row.			

Waist Shaping

	[S]/[M]		[M]/[L]
ROW 1 K1, ssk, work Row 1 of Knit Pattern Stitch to last 3 stitches, K2tog, K1. You now have	88 sts	•	100 sts
ROWS 2–5 Work Rows 2–5 of Knit Pattern Stitch.			
ROW 6 Work Row 6 of Knit Pattern Stitch. You now have	44 sts	•	50 sts
ROW 7 Work Row 7 of Knit Pattern Stitch. You now have	88 sts	•	100 sts
ROW 8 P1, ssp, work Row 8 of Knit Pattern Stitch to last 3 stitches, P2tog, P1. You now have	86 sts	•	98 sts

KNITTING THE CARDIGAN (continued)	[S]/[M]		[M]/[L]
ROWS 9–16 Repeat Rows 1–8, including decreases. You now have	82 sts	•	94 sts
ROWS 17–24 Repeat Rows 1–8, including decreases. You now have	78 sts	•	90 sts
ROWS 25–31 Repeat Rows 1–7, including decreases. You now have	76 sts	•	88 sts
ROW 32 Work Row 8 of Knit Pattern Stitch.			
ROWS 33–48 Work Rows 1–8 of Knit Pattern Stitch twice. The piece now measures	6" (15 cm)	•	6" (15 cm)

Small/Medium Only

ROW 49 K1, increase 1, work Row 1 of Knit Pattern Stitch to last 3 stitches, increase 1, K1. You now have	78 sts	•	
ROWS 50–55 Work Rows 2–7 of Knit Pattern Stitch.			
ROW 56 K1, increase 1, work Row 8 of Knit Pattern Stitch to last 3 stitches, increase 1, K1. You now have	80 sts	•	
ROWS 57–64 Repeat Rows 49–56, including increases. You now have	84 sts	•	
ROWS 65–72 Repeat Rows 49–56, including increases. You now have	88 sts	•	
ROW 73 Repeat Row 49, including increases. You now have	90 sts	•	
ROWS 74–80 Work Rows 2–8 of Knit Pattern Stitch.			
ROWS 81–112 Work Rows 1–8 of Knit Pattern Stitch four times. The piece now measures	14" (35 cm)	•	

Medium/Large Only

ROWS 49–56 Work Rows 1–8 of Knit Pattern Stitch, with no decrease. The piece now measures		•	7" (17.5 cm)
ROW 57 K1, increase 1, work Row 1 of Knit Pattern Stitch to last 3 stitches, increase 1, K1. You now have		•	90 sts

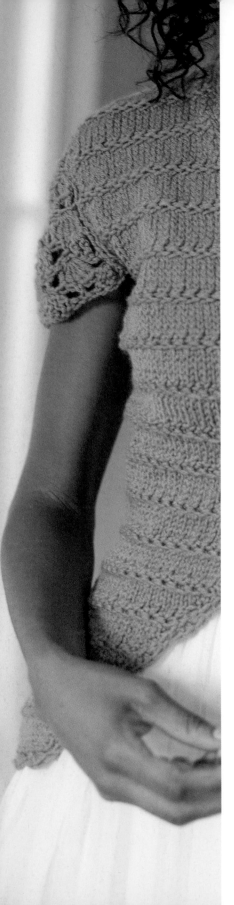

Knit

	[S]/[M]		[M]/[L]
ROWS 58–63 Work Rows 2–7 of Knit Pattern Stitch.			
ROW 64 K1, increase 1, work Row 8 of Knit Pattern Stitch to last 3 stitches, increase 1, K1. You now have		•	92 sts
ROWS 65–72 Repeat Rows 57–64, including increases. You now have		•	96 sts
ROWS 73–80 Repeat Rows 57–64, including increases. You now have		•	100 sts
ROW 81 Repeat Row 57, including increases. You now have		•	102 sts
ROWS 82–88 Work Rows 2–8 of Knit Pattern Stitch.			
ROWS 89–120 Work Rows 1–8 of Knit Pattern Stitch four times. The piece now measures		•	15" (37.5 cm)

Armhole Shaping on Back

	[S]/[M]		[M]/[L]
ROW 1 Bind off	6 sts	•	6 sts
Work remaining stitches in Row 1 of Knit Pattern Stitch. You now have	84 sts	•	96 sts
ROW 2 Bind off	6 sts	•	6 sts
Work remaining stitches in Row 2 of Knit Pattern Stitch. You now have	78 sts	•	90 sts
ROWS 3–8 Work Rows 3–8 of Knit Pattern Stitch.			
ROWS 9–40 Work Rows 1–8 of Knit Pattern Stitch five times. The piece now measures	20" (50 cm)	•	22" (55 cm)

Neck Shaping on Back

	[S]/[M]		[M]/[L]
ROW 1 Continuing in Row 1 of Knit Pattern Stitch, work across	26 sts	•	30 sts
Bind off the middle	26 sts	•	30 sts
Work the final	26 sts	•	30 sts

	[S]/[M]		[M]/[L]
ROWS 2–5 (LEFT SIDE) Work Rows 2–5 of Knit Pattern Stitch, decreasing 1 stitch every row at neck edge. *You now have*	22 sts	•	26 sts
ROWS 6–8 (LEFT SIDE) Work Rows 6–8 of Knit Pattern Stitch. The left side now measures	21" (52.5 cm)	•	23" (57.5 cm)
Bind off all stitches.			
ROWS 2–5 (RIGHT SIDE) Attach yarn to right side. Work Rows 2–5 of Knit Pattern Stitch, decreasing 1 stitch every row at neck edge. *You now have*	22 sts	•	26 sts
ROWS 6–8 (RIGHT SIDE) Work Rows 6–8 of Knit Pattern Stitch. The right side now measures	21" (52.5 cm)	•	23" (57.5 cm)
Bind off all stitches.			

Right Front

	[S]/[M]		[M]/[L]
SET UP Using straight needles, cast on	16 sts	•	22 sts
STARTER ROW (WRONG SIDE) Purl to end of row.			

Right Front Waist Shaping

	[S]/[M]		[M]/[L]
ROW 1 Work Row 1 of Knit Pattern Stitch to last 3 stitches, K2tog, K1. *You now have*	15 sts	•	21 sts
ROW 2 Work Row 2 of Knit Pattern Stitch.			
ROW 3 K1, increase 1, work Row 3 of Knit Pattern Stitch. *You now have*	16 sts	•	22 sts
ROW 4 Work Row 4 of Knit Pattern Stitch.			
ROW 5 K1, increase 1, work Row 5 of Knit Pattern Stitch. *You now have*	17 sts	•	23 sts
ROW 6 K1, work Row 6 of Knit Pattern Stitch. *You now have*	9 sts	•	17 sts
ROW 7 Work Row 7 of Knit Pattern Stitch to last stitch, K1. *You now have*	17 sts	•	23 sts

	[S]/[M]		[M]/[L]
ROW 8 P1, P2tog, work Row 8 of Knit Pattern Stitch to last 2 stitches, increase 1, K1. *You now have*	17 sts	•	23 sts
ROW 9 K1, increase 1, work Row 1 of Knit Pattern Stitch to last 3 stitches, K2tog, K1.			
ROWS 10–16 Repeat Rows 2–8, including increases and decreases. *You now have*	19 sts	•	25 sts
ROW 17 Repeat Row 9.			
ROWS 18–24 Repeat Rows 2–8, including increases and decreases. *You now have*	21 sts	•	27 sts
ROW 25 Repeat Row 9.			
ROWS 26–32 Repeat Rows 2–8, including increases but omitting decrease at beginning of Row 8. *You now have*	24 sts	•	30 sts
ROWS 33–48 Work Rows 1–8 of Knit Pattern Stitch twice, increasing 1 stitch at the beginning of Rows 1, 3, and 5, and at the end of Row 8. *You now have*	32 sts	•	38 sts
The piece now measures	6" (15 cm)	•	6" (15 cm)

Small/Medium Only

	[S]/[M]	
ROW 49 K1, increase 1, work Row 1 of Knit Pattern Stitch to last 2 stitches, increase 1, K1. *You now have*	34 sts	•
ROWS 50–55 Work Rows 2–7 of Knit Pattern Stitch, increasing 1 stitch at beginning of Rows 3 and 5. *You now have*	36 sts	•
ROW 56 P1, increase 1, work Row 8 of Knit Pattern Stitch to last 2 stitches, increase 1, P1. *You now have*	38 sts	•
ROW 57 Repeat Row 49. *You now have*	40 sts	•
ROWS 58–63 Work Rows 2–7 of Knit Pattern Stitch.		
ROW 64 Work Row 8 of Knit Pattern Stitch to last 2 stitches, increase 1, P1. *You now have*	41 sts	•
ROW 65 Work Row 1 of Knit Pattern Stitch to last 2 stitches, increase 1, K1. *You now have*	42 sts	•

	[S]/[M]	[M]/[L]
ROWS 66–71 Work Rows 2–7 of Knit Pattern Stitch.		
ROW 72 Repeat Row 64. *You now have*	43 sts •	
ROW 73 Repeat Row 65. *You now have*	44 sts •	
ROWS 74–80 Work Rows 2–8 of Knit Pattern Stitch.		
ROWS 81–88 Work Rows 1–8 of Knit Pattern Stitch. *The piece now measures*	11" (27.5 cm) •	
ROWS 89–112 Work Rows 1–8 of Knit Pattern Stitch three times, decreasing 1 stitch at beginning of Rows 1 and 5. *You now have*	38 sts •	
The piece now measures	14" (35 cm) •	

Medium/Large Only

	[S]/[M]	[M]/[L]
ROWS 49–56 Work Rows 1–8 of Knit Pattern Stitch, with no decrease. *The piece now measures*	•	7" (17.5 cm)
ROW 57 K1, increase 1, work Row 1 of Knit Pattern Stitch to last 2 stitches, increase 1, K1. *You now have*	•	40 sts
ROWS 58–63 Work Rows 2–7 of Knit Pattern Stitch, increasing 1 stitch at beginning of Rows 3 and 5. *You now have*	•	42 sts
ROW 64 P1, increase 1, work Row 8 of Knit Pattern Stitch to last 2 stitches, increase 1, P1. *You now have*	•	44 sts
ROW 65 Repeat Row 57. *You now have*	•	46 sts
ROWS 66–71 Work Rows 2–7 of Knit Pattern Stitch.		
ROW 72 Work Row 8 of Knit Pattern Stitch to last 2 stitches, increase 1, P1. *You now have*	•	47 sts
ROW 73 Work Row 1 of Knit Pattern Stitch to last 2 stitches, increase 1, K1. *You now have*	•	48 sts
ROWS 74–79 Work Rows 2–7 of Knit Pattern Stitch.		
ROW 80 Repeat Row 72. *You now have*	•	49 sts

KNITTING THE CARDIGAN (continued)

	[S]/[M]		[M]/[L]
ROW 81 Repeat Row 73. You now have		•	50 sts
ROWS 82–88 Work Rows 2–8 of Knit Pattern Stitch.			
ROWS 89–96 Work Rows 1–8 of Knit Pattern Stitch. The piece now measures		•	12" (30 cm)
ROWS 97–120 Work Rows 1–8 of Knit Pattern Stitch three times, decreasing 1 stitch at beginning of Rows 1 and 5. You now have		•	44 sts
The piece now measures		•	15" (37.5 cm)

Right Front Armhole Shaping (Both Sizes)

	[S]/[M]		[M]/[L]
ROW 1 K1, ssk, work Row 1 of Knit Pattern Stitch. You now have	37 sts	•	43 sts
ROW 2 Bind off	6 sts	•	6 sts
Work remaining stitches in Row 2 of Knit Pattern Stitch. You now have	31 sts	•	37 sts
ROWS 3–8 Work Rows 3–8 of Knit Pattern Stitch, decreasing 1 stitch at beginning of Row 5. You now have	30 sts	•	36 sts
ROWS 9–40 Work Rows 1–8 of Knit Pattern Stitch four times, decreasing 1 stitch at beginning of Rows 1 and 5. You now have	22 sts	•	28 sts
ROWS 41–56 Work even in Knit Pattern Stitch. The piece now measures	21" (52.5 cm)	•	23" (57.5 cm)
Bind off all stitches.			

Left Front

	[S]/[M]		[M]/[L]
SET UP Using straight needles, cast on	16 sts	•	22 sts
STARTER ROW (WRONG SIDE) Purl to end of row.			

	[S]/[M]		[M]/[L]

Left Front Waist Shaping

	[S]/[M]		[M]/[L]
ROW 1 K1, ssk, work Row 1 of Knit Pattern Stitch. *You now have*	15 sts	•	21 sts
ROW 2 Work Row 2 of Knit Pattern Stitch.			
ROW 3 Work Row 3 of Knit Pattern Stitch to last 2 stitches, increase 1, K1. *You now have*	16 sts	•	22 sts
ROW 4 Work Row 4 of Knit Pattern Stitch.			
ROW 5 Work Row 5 of Knit Pattern Stitch to last 2 stitches, increase 1, K1. *You now have*	17 sts	•	23 sts
ROW 6 Work Row 6 of Knit Pattern Stitch to last stitch, end K1. *You now have*	9 sts	•	17 sts
ROW 7 K1, work Row 7 of Knit Pattern Stitch. *You now have*	17 sts	•	23 sts
ROW 8 P1, increase 1, work Row 8 of Knit Pattern Stitch to last 3 stitches, P2tog, P1. *You now have*	17 sts	•	23 sts
ROW 9 P1, ssp, work Row 1 of Knit Pattern Stitch to last 2 stitches, increase 1, P1.			
ROWS 10–16 Repeat Rows 2–8, including increases and decreases. *You now have*	19 sts	•	25 sts
ROW 17 Repeat Row 9.			
ROWS 18–24 Repeat Rows 2–8, including increases and decreases. *You now have*	21 sts	•	27 sts
ROW 25 Repeat Row 9.			
ROWS 26–32 Repeat Rows 2–8, including increases but omitting decrease on last stitch of Row 8. *You now have*	24 sts	•	30 sts
ROWS 33–48 Work Rows 1–8 of Knit Pattern Stitch twice, increasing 1 stitch at the beginning of Rows 1, 3, and 5 and at the end of Row 8. *You now have*	32 sts	•	38 sts
The piece now measures	6" (15 cm)	•	6" (15 cm)

KNITTING THE CARDIGAN (continued)

	[S]/[M]	[M]/[L]
Small/Medium Only		
ROW 49 K1, increase 1, work Row 1 of Knit Pattern Stitch to last 2 stitches, increase 1, K1. *You now have*	34 sts	•
ROWS 50–55 Work Rows 2–7 of Knit Pattern Stitch, increasing 1 stitch at end of Rows 3 and 5. *You now have*	36 sts	•
ROW 56 P1, increase 1, work Row 8 of Knit Pattern Stitch to last 2 stitches, increase 1, P1. *You now have*	38 sts	•
ROW 57 Repeat Row 49. *You now have*	40 sts	•
ROWS 58–63 Work Rows 2–7 of Knit Pattern Stitch.		
ROW 64 P1, increase 1, work Row 8 of Knit Pattern Stitch. *You now have*	41 sts	•
ROW 65 Increase 1 stitch, work Row 1 of Knit Pattern Stitch. *You now have*	42 sts	•
ROWS 66–71 Work Rows 2–7 of Knit Pattern Stitch.		
ROW 72 Repeat Row 64. *You now have*	43 sts	•
ROW 73 Repeat Row 65. *You now have*	44 sts	•
ROWS 74–80 Work Rows 2–8 of Knit Pattern Stitch.		
ROWS 81–88 Work Rows 1–8 of Knit Pattern Stitch. *The piece now measures*	11" (27.5 cm)	•
ROWS 89–112 Work Rows 1–8 of Knit Pattern Stitch three times, decreasing 1 stitch at end of Rows 1 and 5. *You now have*	38 sts	•
The piece now measures	14" (35 cm)	•
Medium/Large Only		
ROWS 49–56 Work Rows 1–8 of Knit Pattern Stitch, with no decrease. *The piece now measures*	•	7" (17.5 cm)
ROW 57 K1, increase 1, work Row 1 of Knit Pattern Stitch to last 2 stitches, increase 1, K1. *You now have*	•	40 sts

	[S]/[M]		[M]/[L]
ROWS 58–63 Work Rows 2–7 of Knit Pattern Stitch, increasing 1 stitch at end of Rows 3 and 5. You now have		•	42 sts
ROW 64 P1, increase 1, work Row 8 of Knit Pattern Stitch to last 2 stitches, increase 1, P1. You now have		•	44 sts
ROW 65 Repeat Row 57. You now have		•	46 sts
ROWS 66–71 Work Rows 2–7 of Knit Pattern Stitch.			
ROW 72 P1, increase 1, work Row 8 of Knit Pattern Stitch. You now have		•	47 sts
ROW 73 Increase 1 stitch, work Row 1 of Knit Pattern Stitch. You now have		•	48 sts
ROWS 74–79 Work Rows 2–7 of Knit Pattern Stitch.			
ROW 80 Repeat Row 72. You now have		•	49 sts
ROW 81 Repeat Row 73. You now have		•	50 sts
ROWS 82–88 Work Rows 2–8 of Knit Pattern Stitch.			
ROWS 89–96 Work Rows 1–8 of Knit Pattern Stitch. The piece now measures		•	12" (30 cm)
ROWS 97–120 Work Rows 1–8 of Knit Pattern Stitch three times, decreasing 1 stitch at end of Rows 1 and 5. You now have		•	44 sts
The piece now measures		•	15" (37.5 cm)

Left Front Armhole Shaping (Both Sizes)

	[S]/[M]		[M]/[L]
ROW 1 Bind off 6 stitches, work Row 1 of Knit Pattern Stitch to last 3 stitches, K2tog, K1. You now have	31 sts	•	37 sts
ROWS 2–8 Work Rows 2–8 of Knit Pattern Stitch, decreasing 1 stitch at end of Row 5. You now have	30 sts	•	36 sts
ROWS 9–40 Work Rows 1–8 of Knit Pattern Stitch four times, decreasing 1 stitch at end of Rows 1 and 5. You now have	22 sts	•	28 sts

KNITTING THE CARDIGAN (continued)	[S]/[M]	[M]/[L]
ROWS 41–56 Work even in Knit Pattern Stitch. The piece now measures	21" (52.5 cm)	23" (57.5 cm)
Bind off all stitches.		
FINISH Sew the side and shoulder seams.		

Crocheting the Edging and Sleeves

SET UP With crochet hook, join yarn in the left shoulder seam at neck edge.

ROUND 1 Sc in first 2 stitches, then sc 2 stitches together across Neck Edge of Left Front. Sc down open edge of Left Front, working 1 sc at every Row 6 of the knitted pattern and 3 sc in between. For Bottom Edge, sc the first 2 stitches, then sc 2 stitches together across Bottom Edge. Work open edge of Right Front as for Left Front. Work sc along Neck Edge of Right Front as for Left Front. Join with a slip stitch when you reach starting point.

ROUND 2 * Skip 1 stitch, work 3 dc in back loop of next stitch, skip 1 stitch, work slip stitch in back loop of next stitch; repeat from * until you reach starting point. Join with a slip stitch. Draw yarn through to fasten off, then break yarn.

Left Armhole Edging

SET UP With crochet hook, join yarn in the left underarm seam.

Work sc around armhole edge, working 1 sc at every Row 6 of the knitted pattern and 3 sc in between. When you reach starting point, join with a slip stitch. Draw yarn through to fasten off, and break yarn. *You now have*	68 sts	76 sts

Right Armhole Edging

SET UP With crochet hook, join yarn in the right underarm seam.

Work same as Left Armhole Edging. *You now have*	68 sts	76 sts

Left Shell Sleeve

SET UP With crochet hook, join yarn to a single crochet stitch (Joining Stitch) of Armhole Edging at left shoulder seam.

NOTE *In the instructions below, "make 1 shell" is done by working 5 tr into a dc.*

ROW 1 Ch 4, skip 3 sc of Armhole Edging, 1 hdc in fourth sc of Armhole Edging, turn, (1 tr, ch 1, * 2 tr, ch 1; repeat from * two more times) into Joining Stitch, ch 1, 1 hdc in fourth sc of Armhole Edging on opposite side of Joining Stitch, ch 4, turn.

ROW 2 4 tr into hdc, ch 1, 1 dc in ch-1 space, (3 tr, ch 1, 3 tr) in next ch-1 space, 1 dc in next ch-1 space, ch 1, 5 tr into hdc, ch 4, turn.

ROW 3 2 tr into first tr of shell, ch 1, 1 dc into third tr of shell (middle of shell), ch 1, make 1 shell, ch 1, 1 dc in next ch-1 space, ch 1, make 1 shell, ch 1, 1 dc into middle of shell, ch 1, 3 tr into top of ch-4, ch 4, turn.

ROW 4 * Make 1 shell, 1 dc into middle of shell; repeat from * once more, make 1 shell, 1 tr into top of ch-4, ch 4, turn.

ROW 5 Work 2 tr into base of ch-4, * ch 1, 1 dc into middle of shell, ch 1, make 1 shell; repeat from * once more, ch 1, 1 dc into middle of shell, ch 1, 3 tr into ch-4, ch 4, turn.

ROW 6 * Make 1 shell, ch 1, 1 dc into middle of shell, ch 1; repeat from * once, make 1 shell, 1 tr into ch-4, ch 4, turn.

ROW 7 Work 2 tr into base of ch-4, ch 1, 1 dc into middle of shell, ch 1, make 1 shell, 1 dc into middle of shell, make 1 shell, ch 1, 1 dc into middle of shell, ch 1, 3 tr into ch-4, ch 4, turn.

ROW 8 Repeat Row 4.

ROW 9 Repeat Row 5.

Break yarn. Tack shell sleeve to armhole edge.

Right Shell Sleeve

SET UP With crochet hook, join yarn to a single crochet stitch (Joining Stitch) of Armhole Edging at right shoulder seam.

ROWS 1–9 Same as Left Shell Sleeve.

Finish

① With crochet hook, join yarn to Left Front at the widest part of the waist. Ch 6, sc in second loop from hook and in each chain, 5 sc. Draw yarn through to fasten off, leaving a 6" (15 cm) tail.

② Use the tail to sew the loose end of the loop to the Left Front close to the beginning of the 5 sc. Use matching thread to sew button opposite on the Right Front.

Dressed-Up Tank Top

Soft and romantic, this updated version of "fillet" crochet (think your granny's tablecloth) is a perfect compliment to your wardrobe. Simple rib stitch and a wool/cotton yarn keep the knit body snug, while the crochet top and bottom provide a touch of texture. The only challenge here is in learning to read the fillet chart, but once that's mastered, the project's a breeze.

Sizes and Finished Measurements
Small/Medium 34" (90 cm)
Medium/Large 40" (1 m)

Yarn
Knit Rowan Wool Cotton, 50% merino wool/50% cotton, 1¾ oz (50 g)/ 123 yds (113 m)
MC = 3 (4) balls #933 Violet
Crochet Rowan 4-ply Cotton, 100% cotton, 1¾ oz (50 g)/ 186 yds (170 m)
CC = 3 (4) balls #136 Bluebell

Tools
Knit US #6 (4 mm) straight needles, or size you need to obtain correct gauge
Crochet Size D/3 (3.25 mm) crochet hook, or size you need to obtain correct gauge

Gauge
Knit 22 sts and 30 rows = 4" × 4" (10 cm × 10 cm) in Knit Pattern Stitch
Crochet 22 sts = 4" (10 cm) in sc

Other Supplies
Large-eye yarn needle

Abbreviations
CC = contrasting color
ch = chain (verb)
ch- = chained loop or chained space
dc = double crochet
K2tog = knit 2 together
MC = main color
sc = single crochet
ssk = slip, slip, knit these 2 stitches together
ssp = slip, slip, purl these 2 stitches together

Pattern Stitch

Filet Pattern Stitch

ROW 1 (RIGHT SIDE) Ch 5, skip 2 stitches, 1 dc into next stitch, * ch 2, skip 2 stitches, 1 dc into each of the next 4 stitches, (ch 2, skip 2 stitches, 1 dc into next stitch) twice; repeat from *, ending last repeat with skip 2 stitches, 1 dc in last stitch. Turn.

ROW 2 Ch 5 (counts as 1 dc, ch 2), skip 2 stitches, 1 dc into next stitch, * 2 dc into next ch-2 space, 1 dc into next stitch, (ch 2, skip 2 stitches, 1 dc into next stitch) twice, 2 dc into next ch-2 space, 1 dc into next stitch, (ch 2, skip 2 stitches, 1 dc into next stitch) twice, 2 dc into next ch-2 space, 1 dc into next stitch, ch 2, skip 2 stitches, 1 dc into next stitch; repeat from * to end of row, ending last repeat with 1 dc in last stitch. Turn.

ROW 3 Ch 3 (counts as 1 dc), skip first stitch, 2 dc into next ch-2 space, 1 dc into next stitch, * (ch 2, skip 2 stitches, 1 dc into next stitch) twice, 2 dc into next space, 1 dc into next stitch, ch 2, skip 2 dc, 1 dc into next stitch, work Embossed Flower (see below) in space just made, 2 dc into next ch-2 space, 1 dc into next stitch, (ch 2, skip 2 stitches, 1 dc into next stitch) twice, 2 dc into next ch-2 space, 1 dc into next stitch; repeat from *, ending last repeat in third chain. Turn.

EMBOSSED FLOWER (WORKED IN ROW 3 OF FILET PATTERN STITCH) Hold work right-side up, treating the stitches that form the four sides of the space as if they were the base ring of the motif. Insert hook through center of "ring" and work 1 sc in top left corner. Working counterclockwise down left side of ring, * ch 3, 3 dc into ring, ch 3, sc in lower left corner; repeat from * three more times, moving from corner to corner, ending with a slip stitch in first sc, then slip stitch to last dc of main pattern.

ROW 4 Repeat Row 2.

ROW 5 Ch 5, skip two chains, 1 dc into next stitch, ch 2, skip 2 stitches, 1 dc into next stitch, * 2 dc into next ch-2 space, 1 dc into next stitch, (ch 2, skip 2 stitches, 1 dc into next stitch) three times; repeat from *, ending last repeat 1 dc in third chain of beginning ch 5. Turn.

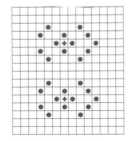

Chart for Larger Size

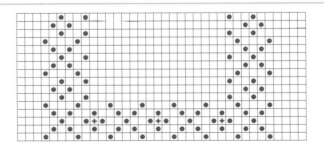

Chart for Bottom Repeat (both sizes)

Pattern Stitch

Knit Pattern Stitch

ROW 1 (WRONG SIDE) * P1, K1; repeat from * to end of row, ending P1.

ROW 2 Knit across row.

Knitting the Tank Top

	[S]/[M]		[M]/[L]

Back

SET UP Using MC and straight needles, cast on	93 sts	•	110 sts
ROW 1 Work Row 1 of Knit Pattern Stitch.			
ROW 2 Work Row 2 of Knit Pattern Stitch.			
NEXT ROWS Work even in Knit Pattern Stitch until measurement of piece from cast-on row is	8½" (21.25 cm)	•	10½" (26.25 cm)
End on wrong-side row.			

Shape Underarms

NEXT 2 ROWS Bind off 6 stitches in Knit Pattern Stitch at beginning of each row, work rest of row in Knit Pattern Stitch. You now have	81 sts	•	94 sts
NEXT ROW K1, ssk, work in Knit Pattern Stitch to last 3 stitches, K2tog, K1. You now have	79 sts	•	92 sts
NEXT ROW P1, ssp, work in Knit Pattern Stitch to last 3 stitches, K2tog, P1. You now have	77 sts	•	90 sts

Medium/Large Only

NEXT ROW K1, ssk, work in Knit Pattern Stitch to last 3 stitches, K2tog, K1. You now have		•	88 sts

KNITTING THE TANK TOP (continued)	[S]/[M]		[M]/[L]
NEXT ROWS (BOTH SIZES) Work even in Knit Pattern Stitch until measurement of piece from cast-on row is	11" (27.5 cm)	•	14" (35 cm)

Small/Medium Only

NEXT ROW Decrease 1 stitch in last row. You now have	76 sts	•	

Both Sizes

Bind off all stitches in Knit Pattern Stitch.

Front

Using MC and straight needles, cast on	93 sts	•	110 sts
Work same as for Back until measurement of piece from cast-on row is	10½" (26.25 cm)	•	13½" (33.75 cm)
Bind off all stitches in Knit Pattern Stitch.			

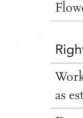

Crocheting the Front Yoke

	[S]/[M]		[M]/[L]
SET UP With right side of Knit Front facing you, using CC and crochet hook, attach yarn to top edge at left underarm. Work 1 sc in each stitch across top edge, ch 2, turn. You now have	76 sts	•	88 sts
STARTER ROW Inserting hook in front loops only, 1 sc in each sc across row. Turn.			
ROWS 1–5 Referring to chart for each size, work rows 1–5 of Filet Pattern Stitch, making three Embossed Flowers in Row 3, as noted.			

Right Shoulder Strap

Work Rows 6–16 of chart, crocheting filets and meshes as established, until measurement from underarm is	8½" (21.25 cm)	•	9½" (23.75 cm)
Draw yarn through last stitch to fasten off, then break yarn.			

Left Shoulder Strap

Join yarn to left top edge of Front. Work in reverse of right shoulder strap, referring to chart for placement of filets and meshes. Draw yarn through last stitch to fasten off, then break yarn.

Crocheting the Back Yoke

Repeat as for Front Yoke.

Crocheting the Edging

Armholes

ROUND 1 With right side of garment facing you, attach CC at underarm. Work sc evenly around edge of armhole, join with slip stitch to first sc, ch 1, turn.

ROUND 2 Inserting hook in front loops only, 1 sc in each sc all around, join with slip stitch to ch-1. Draw yarn through last stitch to fasten off, then break yarn.

Finish other armhole in same way.

Neckline

Work two rounds of sc around neckline, following instructions for Rounds 1 and 2 for Armholes.

Crocheting the Bottom Band

	[S]/[M]	[M]/[L]
SET UP With right side of garment facing you, attach CC to bottom edge at side seam. Sc around bottom edge. Do not join. Ch 1, turn. *You now have*	201 sts	226 sts

STARTER ROUND Inserting hook in front loops only, 1 sc in each sc all around. Turn.

ROUNDS 1–5 Referring to chart for bottom band, work Rows 1–5 of Fillet Pattern Stitch, working eight Embossed Flowers in Round 3, as noted. Draw yarn through last stitch to fasten off, then break yarn.

Sew the ends of the Bottom Band together.

Finish

Place Front and Back together with right sides facing. Using MC and yarn needle, sew side seams. With CC and yarn needle, sew shoulder seams.

Openwork V-Neck Cardigan

Show off your talent with this unique cardigan. The crochet body is worked in a worsted-weight wool to keep it quick, although the shaping slows you down a little. Deep knitted ribbing on the bottom and sleeves are a perfect compliment to the open crochet. Once you get in the rhythm of the pattern you will surely be able to sing its praises.

Sizes and Chest Measurements
Small/Medium 36" (90 m)
Medium/Large 40" (1 m)

Yarn
Cascade 220, 100% wool,
   3.5 oz (100 g)/220 yds (208 m)
7 (9) skeins #8686 Brown

Tools
Knit US #8 (5 mm) straight needles, or size
   you need to obtain correct gauge
Crochet Size H/8 (5 mm) crochet hook, or
   size you need to obtain correct gauge

Gauge
Knit 16 sts and 18 rows = 4" × 4"
   (10 cm × 10 cm) in Stockinette Stitch
Crochet 2 shells = 3½" (8.8 cm);
   9 rows = 4"(10 cm) in Crochet
   Pattern Stitch

Other Supplies
Large-eye yarn needle
Straight pins
Five ¾" (1.8 cm) buttons
Matching sewing thread and needle

Abbreviations
ch = chain (verb)
ch- = chained loop or chained space
dc = double crochet
hdc = half double crochet
sc = single crochet
ssk = slip, slip, knit these 2 stitches
   together
tr = treble crochet

Pattern Stitch

Crochet Pattern Stitch

ROW 1 (RIGHT SIDE) * 1 sc in first stitch, ch 5, skip 5 stitches; repeat from * across row, ending 1 sc in last stitch, ch 1, turn.

ROW 2 1 sc in same stitch as ch-1, * (1 hdc, 1 dc, 1 tr, 1 dc, 1 hdc) in ch-5 space, 1 sc in sc; repeat from * across row, ending 1 sc in sc, ch 3, turn.

ROW 3 * 1 sc in tr of previous row, ch 5; repeat from * across row, ending 1 sc in tr, ch 3, 1 sc in last sc, ch 4, turn. (Ch 4 is same as tr.)

ROW 4 (1 dc, 1 hdc) in ch-3 space, * 1 sc in sc, (1 hdc, 1 dc, 1 tr, 1 dc, 1 hdc) in ch-5 space; repeat from * across row, ending 1 sc in sc, (1 hdc, 1 dc, 1 tr) in ch-3 space, ch 5, turn.

ROW 5 * Sc in center tr, ch 5; repeat from *, ending sc in top of fourth chain from previous row, ch 1, turn.

Repeat Rows 2–5 for Crochet Pattern Stitch.

Knitting the Deep Rib

Front and Back

	[S]/[M]	[M]/[L]
SET UP Using straight needles, cast on	171 sts	183 sts
ROW 1 * K1, P1; repeat from * to end of row, ending K1.		
ROW 2 * P1, K1; repeat from * to end of row, ending P1.		
Repeat Rows 1 and 2 until ribbing measures	8" (20 cm)	9" (22.5 cm)
DECREASE ROW (RIGHT SIDE) Working in ribbing, make 14 ssk decreases evenly spaced across row. For each ssk, let purl stitch be the first stitch you slip to right needle. *You now have*	157 sts	169 sts
Bind off in knit stitch.		

Crocheting the Top

	[S]/[M]	[M]/[L]
SET UP Using crochet hook, attach yarn to bound-off edge on wrong side of left front. Work 1 sc in each stitch to end of row. Ch 1, turn.		
ROWS 1 AND 2 Work Rows 1 and 2 of Crochet Pattern Stitch. You now have	26 full shells	28 full shells
ROWS 3 AND 4 Work Rows 3 and 4 of Crochet Pattern Stitch.		
NEXT ROWS Repeat Rows 2–5 of Crochet Pattern Stitch. End ready for Row 5 when work measures approximately	8" (20 cm)	9" (22.5 cm)

Right Front

	[S]/[M]	[M]/[L]
ROW 1 1 sc in sc, ch 3 (decrease made), 1 sc in tr, * ch 5, 1 sc in tr; repeat from *	5 times	6 times
Including the ch-3 loop, you now have	6 loops	7 loops
ROW 2 Work Row 2 of Crochet Pattern Stitch on these stitches only, ending (1 hdc, 1 dc, 1 tr) into ch-3 loop. You now have one half shell and	5 full shells	6 full shells
ROW 3 Work Row 3 of Crochet Pattern Stitch.		
ROW 4 Work Row 4 of Crochet Pattern Stitch.		
ROWS 5–12 Repeat Rows 1–4 twice more. You now have one half shell and	3 full shells	4 full shells
Work even until crochet section, measured from end of deep rib, is	16½" (41.25 cm)	18" (45 cm)

Back

	[S]/[M]	[M]/[L]
SET UP Attach yarn to Front and Back piece by skipping 1 shell for underarm and attaching yarn to next stitch.		
ROW 1 Work Row 5 of Crochet Pattern Stitch across	12 shells	12 shells
NEXT ROWS Work even until crochet section, measured from end of deep rib, is	16½" (41.25 cm)	18" (45 cm)

CROCHETING THE TOP (continued)
Left Front

	[S]/[M]	[M]/[L]
SET UP Attach yarn to Front and Back piece by skipping 1 shell for underarm and attaching yarn to next stitch. To left of yarn join, you now have	6 full shells	7 full shells
ROW 1 1 sc in same stitch as join, * ch 5, 1 sc in tr; repeat from * to end of row, ending 1 sc in tr, ch 3 (decrease made), 1 sc in sc. Including the ch-3 loop, you now have	6 loops	7 loops
ROW 2 1 sc in sc, (1 hdc, 1 dc, 1 tr) into ch-3 loop, * 1 sc in sc, (1 hdc, 1 dc, 1 tr, 1 dc, 1 hdc) into ch-5 loop; repeat from *	4 times	5 times
You now have one half shell and	5 full shells	6 full shells
ROW 3 Work Row 3 of Crochet Pattern Stitch.		
ROW 4 Work Row 4 of Crochet Pattern Stitch.		
ROWS 5–12 Repeat Rows 1–4 twice more. You now have one half shell and	3 full shells	4 full shells
Work even until crochet section measures	16½" (41.25 cm)	18" (45 cm)

Knitting the Deep Rib for Sleeve (make 2)

	[S]/[M]	[M]/[L]
SET UP Using straight needles, cast on	40 sts	46 sts
ROW 1 * K1, P1; repeat from * across row, ending K1.		
ROW 2 * P1, K1; repeat from * across row, ending P1.		
Repeat Rows 1 and 2 until ribbing measures	4" (10 cm)	4" (10 cm)
INCREASE ROW (RIGHT SIDE) Working in ribbing, increase evenly across the Row	15 sts	21 sts
NOTE Increase by knitting into the front and the back of a stitch.		
You now have	55 sts	67 sts
Bind off in knit stitch.		

then Crochet

Crocheting the Sleeve Top

	[S]/[M]	[M]/[L]
SET UP Using crochet hook, attach yarn to bound-off edge on wrong side of sleeve. 1 sc in each stitch to end of row, ch 1, turn.		
ROW 1 Work Row 1 of Crochet Pattern Stitch. You now have	9 loops	11 loops
ROWS 2–4 Work Rows 2–4 of Crochet Pattern Stitch.		
Work even in Crochet Pattern Stitch until sleeve measures	20" (50 cm)	21" (52.5 cm)
LAST ROW End on Row 3 or Row 5. 1 sc in each ch and each sc. Repeat for second sleeve.		

Crocheting the Neck Edging

ROW 1 Using crochet hook, join yarn to bottom corner of Left Front. With wrong side facing, work sc up edge of left front, around back neck, and down right front, ch 1, turn.		
Use pins to mark edge of Right Front between lower edge and neck shaping for	5 buttonholes	6 buttonholes
Marks should be evenly spaced about 2¼" (5.6 cm) apart.		
ROW 2 With right side facing you, (1 sc in each sc) twice, * (ch 1, skip 1: one buttonhole made), 1 sc in each sc to next buttonhole marking; repeat from *	4 more times	5 more times
Continue working 1 sc in each sc to bottom of left edge, ch 1, turn.		
ROW 3 Work 1 sc in each sc. Break off yarn.		
Using matching thread, sew buttons onto Left Right Front opposite buttonholes.		

Finish

① Using yarn needle, sew shoulder seams.

② Sew sleeve seams, leaving 1" (2.5 cm) open at the underarm.

③ Set sleeves into Back and Front piece and sew in place. (See illustration on page 89.)

Designer Jacket

Victorian influence and a modern feel come together in this subtly hued top. The ribbon yarn adds to the charm of the basic knit bodice and sleeves and gives it a soft sheen. Crochet the peplum and sleeve detail in a shell stitch that is easy to shape and helps to create the feeling of yesteryear. Think romantic picnic in the park!

Sizes and Finished Chest Measurements
Small 38" (96 cm)
Medium 40½" (103 cm)
Large 42½" (108 cm)

Yarn
K1, C2 Italian Ice, 61% cotton/26% linen/13% viscose, 1.75 oz (50 g)/ 76 yds (70 m)
MC = 8 (9, 10) skeins #120 Vanilla
K1, C2 Tartelette, 50% cotton/40% tactel/10% nylon, 1.75 oz (50 g)/ 76 yds (70 m)
CC = 4 (5, 6) skeins #211 Pink Grapefruit

Tools
Knit US #9 (5.5 mm) straight needles, or size you need to obtain correct gauge
Crochet Size H/8 (5 mm) crochet hook, or size you need to obtain correct gauge

Gauge
Knit 17 sts and 24 rows = 4" × 4" (10 cm × 10 cm) in Stockinette Stitch
Crochet 2 shells = 3" (7.5 cm); 7 rows = 4" (10 cm) in Peplum

Other Supplies
Large-eye yarn needle
Straight pins
5 (5, 6) small pearl buttons
Matching sewing thread and needle

Abbreviations
CC = contrasting color
ch = chain (verb)
ch- = chained loop or chained space
dc = double crochet
MC = main color
P2tog = purl 2 together
psso = pass slipped stitch over
sc = single crochet
St st = stockinette stitch

Knit

Knitting the Cardigan

	[S]		[M]		[L]
Back					
SET UP Using MC and straight needles, cast on	62 sts	•	64 sts	•	68 sts
ROW 1 (WRONG SIDE) Purl to end of row.					
ROW 2 K1, increase 1, knit to last 2 stitches, increase 1, K1. You now have	64 sts	•	66 sts	•	70 sts
ROWS 3–22 Repeat Rows 1 and 2	10 times	•	10 times	•	10 times
You now have	84 sts	•	86 sts	•	90 sts
NEXT ROWS Work even until piece measures	5½" (13.75 cm)	•	6" (15 cm)	•	7" (17.5 cm)
NEXT 2 ROWS Bind off first 7 stitches, continue in St st to end of row. You now have	70 sts	•	72 sts	•	76 sts
NEXT ROWS Work even in St st until piece measures	13½" (33.75 cm)	•	14" (35 cm)	•	15½" (38.75 cm)
NEXT ROW Work across	20 sts	•	21 sts	•	23 sts
Bind off next 30 stitches.					
Work across last	20 sts	•	21 sts	•	23 sts
NEXT ROWS Work 1 row on last group of stitches. Bind off.					
Join yarn to other group of stitches. Work 1 row. Bind off.					
Right Front					
SET UP Using MC and straight needles, cast on	31 sts	•	32 sts	•	34 sts
ROW 1 (WRONG SIDE) Purl to end of row.					
ROW 2 Knit to last 2 stitches, increase 1, K1. You now have	32 sts	•	33 sts	•	35 sts

KNITTING THE CARDIGAN (continued)	[S]		[M]		[L]
ROWS 3–22 Repeat Rows 1 and 2	10 times		10 times		10 times
You now have	42 sts	•	43 sts	•	45 sts
NEXT ROWS Work even until piece measures	5½" (13.75 cm)	•	6" (15 cm)	•	7" (17.5 cm)
End on a right-side row.					
NEXT ROW (WRONG SIDE) Bind off first 7 stitches. Continue in St st to end of row. You now have	35 sts	•	36 sts	•	38 sts
NEXT ROWS Work even in St st until piece measures	9½" (23.75 cm)	•	10" (25 cm)	•	10½" (26.25 cm)

Neck Shaping (right side)

ROW 1 K2, slip 1, K1, psso, knit to end of row.

ROW 2 Purl across row to last 4 stitches, P2tog, P2.

	[S]		[M]		[L]
NEXT ROWS Repeat Rows 1 and 2, decreasing 1 stitch at neck edge every row and working even in St st, for	12 rows	•	13 rows	•	13 rows
You now have	20 sts	•	21 sts	•	23 sts
Work even in St st until piece measures	14" (35 cm)	•	14" (35 cm)	•	16" (40 cm)

Bind off.

Left Front

	[S]		[M]		[L]
SET UP Using MC and straight needles, cast on	31 sts	•	32 sts	•	34 sts
ROW 1 (WRONG SIDE) Purl to end of row.					
ROW 2 K1, increase 1, knit to end of row. You now have	32 sts	•	33 sts	•	35 sts

KNITTING THE CARDIGAN (continued)	[S]		[M]		[L]
ROWS 3–22 Repeat Rows 1 and 2	10 times	•	10 times	•	10 times
You now have	42 sts	•	43 sts	•	45 sts
NEXT ROWS Work even until piece measures	5½" (13.75 cm)	•	6" (15 cm)	•	7" (17.5 cm)
End on a wrong-side row.					
NEXT ROW (WRONG SIDE) Bind off first 7 stitches. Continue in St st to end of row. You now have	35 sts	•	36 sts	•	38 sts
NEXT ROWS Work even in St st until piece measures	9½" (23.75 cm)	•	10" (25 cm)	•	10½" (26.25 cm)

Neck Shaping (right side)

	[S]		[M]		[L]
ROW 1 Knit to last 4 stitches, slip 1, K1, psso, K2.					
ROW 2 P2, P2tog, purl to end of row.					
NEXT ROWS Repeat Rows 1 and 2, decreasing 1 stitch at neck edge every row and working even in St st for	12 rows	•	13 rows	•	13 rows
You now have	20 sts	•	21 sts	•	23 sts
Work even in St st until piece measures	14" (35 cm)	•	14" (35 cm)	•	16" (40 cm)

Bind off.

Sleeves (make 2)

	[S]		[M]		[L]
SET UP Using MC and straight needles, cast on	40 sts	•	42 sts	•	44 sts
ROW 1 (WRONG SIDE) Purl to end of row.					
ROW 2 Knit to end of row.					
ROW 3 P1, increase 1, purl to last 2 stitches, increase 1, P1. You now have	42 sts	•	44 sts	•	46 sts

KNITTING THE CARDIGAN (continued)	[S]		[M]		[L]
ROW 4 Knit to end of row.					
ROW 5 Purl to end of row.					
ROW 6 K1, increase 1, knit to last 2 stitches, increase 1, K1. *You now have*	44 sts	•	46 sts	•	48 sts
NEXT ROWS In the next rows, you will be working even in St st and increasing 1 stitch at each edge every third row, as follows: Repeat Rows 1–6	7 times	•	7 times	•	7 times
and Rows 1–3	once	•	(no more)	•	once
You now have	74 sts	•	74 sts	•	78 sts
Work even in St st until piece measures	11" (27.5 cm)	•	12" (30 cm)	•	13" (32.5 cm)
Bind off.					

Finish

① Using MC and yarn needle, sew shoulder and side seams.

② Sew each sleeve seam, leaving 1" (2.5 cm) open at underarm.

③ Set sleeves into body. (See illustration on page 89.)

Crocheting the Edging

Front and Neck Edges

SET UP Using MC and crochet hook, join yarn to bottom right corner.

ROW 1 1 sc into every other row up right front edge, 3 sc at corner, * (1 sc in next stitch) twice, skip 1 stitch; repeat from * along neck decrease edge; 1 sc into every other row; * (1 sc in next stitch) twice, skip 1 stitch; repeat from * along back neck edge; 1 sc into every other row; * (1 sc in next stitch) twice, skip 1 stitch; repeat from * along neck decrease edge, 3 sc at top corner, 1 sc into every row down left front edge. Ch 1, turn.

ROW 2 (BUTTON BAND) Sc in each sc, draw yarn through to fasten off at beginning of neck decreases, then break off yarn.

ROW 2 (BUTTONHOLES) Use straight pins to mark edge of right front for 5 buttonholes for small and medium sizes and 6 buttonholes for large size.

Join yarn to right front at beginning of neck decreases. Work (1 sc in 1 stitch) twice, * (ch 1, skip 1: buttonhole made), 1 sc in each sc to next buttonhole marker; repeat from * to bottom edge. Break yarn.

Sleeve Edges

SET UP Using CC and crochet hook, join yarn to lower sleeve edge at seam.

STARTER ROUND 31 sc around, ch 3, turn.

Join Tartelette yarn at seam. 31 sc around, ch 3, turn.

ROW 1 * Skip 2, 5 dc in next sc, skip 2, 1 dc in next dc; repeat from *, end by skipping 2 sc, slip stitch to third chain of ch-3, ch 3, turn.

ROW 2 2 dc in base of ch-3, * 1 dc in third dc of shell, 5 dc in next dc, 1 dc in third dc of shell, 3 dc in dc; repeat from * once more, ending with 1 dc in third dc of shell, join with slip stitch to third chain of ch-3, ch 3, turn.

ROW 3 * 5 dc in dc, 1 dc in third dc of shell, 3 dc in dc, 1 dc in third dc of shell; repeat once more from *, ending with slip stitch to ch-3. Draw yarn through to fasten off, then break yarn.

Crocheting the Peplum

SET UP Using CC and crochet hook, join yarn to lower edge of right front.

STARTER ROW * 1 sc in stitch twice, skip 1 stitch; repeat from * across lower edge, ch 1, turn.

ROW 1 * Dc, skip 2, 5 dc in next sc, skip 2; repeat from * across, ch 1, turn.

ROW 2 3 dc in first dc, * 1 dc in middle dc of shell, 5 dc in dc; repeat from * across, ending with 3 dc in dc, ch 3, turn.

ROW 3 (5 dc in dc, 1 dc in middle dc of shell) twice, (7 dc in dc, 1 dc in middle dc of shell) three times, (5 dc in dc, 1 dc in middle dc of shell) four times, (7 dc in dc, 1 dc in middle dc of shell) three times.

ROW 4 3 dc in first dc, 1 dc in middle dc of shell, (5 dc in dc, 1 dc in middle dc of shell) once, (7 dc in dc, 1 dc in middle dc of shell) three times, (5 dc in dc, 1 dc in middle dc of shell) five times, (7 dc in dc, 1 dc in middle dc of shell) three times, (5 dc in dc, 1 dc in middle dc of shell) once, end 3 dc in dc, ch 3, turn.

ROW 5 Same as Row 3.

ROW 6 Same as Row 4.

ROW 7 Same as Row 3, but do not ch 3 or turn. Draw yarn through last stitch to fasten off, then break yarn.

Berries and Buttons Sweater

What little girl wouldn't love to dress up in her ballerina best with this charming sweater to top it off. White is the perfect color to show off the red crochet cherries. Deep crochet edging makes the basic knit cardigan special, inspiring your little ballerina to dance around the room.

Sizes and Finished Measurements
Size 2 24" (61 cm) chest;
13" (32.5 cm) long
Size 4 26" (66 cm) chest; 14" (35 cm) long
Size 6 28" (71 cm) chest; 15"
(37.5 cm) long

Yarn
Patons Classic Merino Wool, 100% wool,
3.5 oz (100 g)/223 yds (205 m)
MC = 2 (2, 3) balls #202 Aran
Patons Grace, 100% cotton,
1.75 oz (50 g)/136 yd (125 m)
CC = 1 ball #60705 Cardinal

Tools
Knit US #8 (5mm) straight needles, or size
you need to obtain correct gauge
Crochet Size H/8 (5mm) crochet hook, for
wool yarn, or size you need to obtain
correct gauge
Size F/5 (4 mm) crochet hook, for cotton
yarn, or size you need to obtain correct
gauge

Gauge
Knit 19 sts and 24 rows = 4" × 4"
(10 cm × 10 cm) in Stockinette Stitch
Crochet 16 sc = 4" (10 cm) using wool yarn
20 sc = 4" (10 cm) using cotton yarn

Other Supplies
Large-eye yarn needle
Straight pins
1 skein light green perle cotton
Blunt-tipped embroidery needle

Abbreviations
CC = contrasting color
ch = chain (verb)
ch- = chained loop or chained space
dc = double crochet
K2tog = knit 2 together
MC = main color
P2tog = purl 2 together
psso = pass slipped stitch over
sc = single crochet
St st = stockinette stitch
yo = yarn over

Knit

Knitting the Sweater

	[Size 2]	[Size 4]	[Size 6]

NOTE To "increase 1," knit into the front and the back of the next stitch.

Back

	[Size 2]		[Size 4]		[Size 6]
SET UP Using MC and straight needles, cast on	58 sts	•	62 sts	•	66 sts
ROWS 1 AND 2 Purl to end of row.					
ROW 3 (RIGHT SIDE) Knit to end of row.					
ROW 4 Purl to end of row.					
Repeat Rows 3 and 4, working even in St st until piece measures	11" (27.5 cm)	•	12" (30 cm)	•	13" (32.5 cm)
Bind off all stitches.					

Right Front

	[Size 2]		[Size 4]		[Size 6]
SET UP Using MC and straight needles, cast on	26 sts	•	28 sts	•	30 sts
ROWS 1 AND 2 Purl to end of row.					
ROW 3 (RIGHT SIDE) Knit to end of row.					
ROW 4 Purl to end of row.					
Repeat Rows 3 and 4, working even in St st until piece measures	8" (20 cm)	•	9" (22.5 cm)	•	10" (25 cm)

Neck Shaping

	[Size 2]		[Size 4]		[Size 6]
ROW 1 (RIGHT SIDE) Bind off first 4 stitches, knit to end of row. You now have	22 sts	•	24 sts	•	26 sts
ROWS 2 AND 4 Purl across row, end P2tog, P1.					

KNITTING THE SWEATER (continued)	[Size 2]		[Size 4]		[Size 6]
ROWS 3 AND 5 K1, slip 1, K1, psso, knit to end of row.					
ROW 6 Purl to end of row.					
NEXT ROWS Repeat Rows 5 and 6	0 times	•	1 time	•	2 times
You now have	18 sts	•	19 sts	•	20 sts
NEXT ROWS Work even in St st until piece measures	11" (27.5 cm)	•	12" (30 cm)	•	13" (32.5 cm)
Bind off all stitches.					

Left Front

	[Size 2]		[Size 4]		[Size 6]
SET UP Using MC and straight needles, cast on	26 sts	•	28 sts	•	30 sts
ROWS 1 AND 2 Purl to end of row.					
ROW 3 (RIGHT SIDE) Knit to end of row.					
ROW 4 Purl to end of row.					
Repeat Rows 3 and 4, working even in St st until piece measures	8" (20 cm)	•	9" (22.5 cm)	•	10" (25 cm)

Neck Shaping

	[Size 2]		[Size 4]		[Size 6]
ROW 1 (WRONG SIDE) Working in St st, bind off first 4 stitches, purl to end of row. *You now have*	22 sts	•	24 sts	•	26 sts
ROWS 2 AND 4 Knit across row, end K2tog, K1.					
ROWS 3 AND 5 P1, P2tog, purl to end of row.					
ROW 6 Knit to end of row.					
NEXT ROWS Repeat Rows 5 and 6	0 times	•	1 time	•	2 times
You now have	18 sts	•	19 sts	•	20 sts

Finish

① Using MC and yarn needle, sew side and shoulder seams.

② Set sleeves into body.

Knit

KNITTING THE SWEATER (continued)	[Size 2]	[Size 4]	[Size 6]
NEXT ROWS Work even in St st until piece measures	11" (27.5 cm)	12" (30 cm)	13" (32.5 cm)
Bind off all stitches.			

Sleeve (make 2)

	[Size 2]	[Size 4]	[Size 6]
SET UP Using MC and straight needles, cast on	27 sts	30 sts	32 sts
ROWS 1 AND 2 Purl to end of row.			
ROW 3 (RIGHT SIDE) Knit to end of row.			
ROW 4 Purl to end of row.			
ROW 5 K1, increase 1, knit to last 2 stitches, end increase 1, K1. *You now have*	29 sts	32 sts	34 sts
ROW 6 Purl to end of row.			
NEXT ROWS Repeat Rows 3–6	4 times	5 times	6 times
You now have	37 sts	42 sts	46 sts
NEXT 6 ROWS Work Rows 3 and 4 twice, Rows 5 and 6 once.			
Repeat last 6 rows three times. *You now have*	45 sts	50 sts	54 sts
NEXT ROWS Work even in St st until piece measures	9" (22.5 cm)	10" (25 cm)	11" (27.5 cm)
Bind off all stitches.			

Crocheting the Cherries and Berries

For the cherry bobbles, using CC and smaller crochet hook, ch 3, * yo, insert hook into third chain from hook and draw up a loop, yo, draw through 2 loops on hook; repeat from * three more times, yo and draw through all 5 loops on hook. Leaving a long tail for sewing, break off yarn.

For the berry buttons, ch 3, join with a slip stitch to form ring.

ROUND 1 6 sc in ring.

ROUND 2 * 1 sc in next sc, 2 sc in next sc; repeat from * to end of round. You now have 9 sc.

DECREASE ROUND * 3 sc together to end of round. Draw yarn through to fasten off, leaving a 6" (15 cm) tail. Make 5 for sizes 2 and 4; make 6 for size 6.

Crocheting the Edging

SET UP Using MC and crochet hook, join yarn to bottom right corner.

ROW 1 1 sc into every other row up right front edge, 3 sc at corner, * (1 sc in next stitch) twice, skip 1 stitch; repeat from * along right neck decrease edge. 1 sc into every other row, (1 sc in next stitch) twice, skip 1 stitch; repeat from * along back neck edge. 1 sc into every other row, (1 sc in next stitch) twice, skip 1 stitch; repeat from * along left neck decrease edge. 3 sc at top corner, 1 sc into every row down left front edge, ch 1, turn.

ROW 2 (BUTTON BAND) Work 1 sc in each sc up left front edge, end at beginning of neck decreases. Draw yarn through last stitch to fasten off, then break yarn.

ROW 2 (BUTTONHOLES) Use pins to mark edge of right front for 5 buttonholes for sizes 2 and 4, and 6 buttonholes for size 6.

Join yarn to bottom right corner. 1 sc in each sc twice, * (ch 1, skip 1: buttonhole made), 1 sc in each sc to next buttonhole marker; repeat from * to beginning of neck shaping. Draw yarn through last stitch to fasten off, then break yarn.

Collar

SET UP Using MC and larger crochet hook, attach yarn to sc at right front neck edge.

ROW 1 Ch 3 (counts as 1 dc), 1 dc in same space (two-thirds shell), * skip 1, 1 dc, skip 1, 3 dc (shell); repeat from * three more times, (1 dc, 3 dc, 1 dc) in 3 stitches at shoulder seam. * Skip 1, 3 dc, skip 1, 1 dc; repeat from * across back, (1 dc, 3 dc, 1 dc) in 3 stitches at shoulder seam, (skip 1, 3 dc, skip 1, 1 dc) twice, skip 1, end 2 dc in last stitch (two-thirds shell), ch 4 (counts as 1 dc and 1 ch), turn.

ROW 2 * Skip 1, 3 dc in dc, skip 1, 1 dc in middle dc of shell; repeat from *, end ch 1, 1 dc in third chain of ch-4, ch 4, turn.

ROW 3 * 1 dc in base of ch-4 (two-thirds shell), skip 1, 1 dc in middle dc of shell, skip 1, 3 dc in dc; repeat from *, end 2 dc in third chain of ch-4 (two-thirds shell), ch 4, turn.

ROW 4 Repeat Row 2.

Draw yarn through last stitch to fasten off, then break yarn.

Edge Trim

SET UP Using CC and smaller crochet hook, attach yarn to bottom front edge of collar.

FINAL ROW * 1 sc in same stitch as join, ch 4, 1 sc in fourth chain from hook, 1 sc in next stitch, ch 1; repeat from * along edge of collar. Break off yarn.

Bottom Band

SET UP Using MC and crochet hook, join yarn to lower edge between two purl rows.

STARTER ROW 1 sc in same stitch as join, * skip 1, 1 sc in next stitch; repeat from * to end of row. Count as you go to make number of sc evenly divisible by 4, ch 3, turn.

ROW 1 * Skip 1, 3 dc in next sc (shell), skip 1, 1 dc in next sc; repeat from * across row, end 3 dc in sc, skip 1, 1 dc in last sc, ch 3, turn.

ROW 2 1 dc in base of ch-3 (two-thirds shell), * skip 1, 1 dc in middle dc of shell, skip 1, 3 dc (shell); repeat from * across row, end 2 dc in last stitch (two-thirds shell), ch 3, turn.

ROW 3 Repeat Row 1.

Edge Trim

SET UP Using CC and smaller crochet hook, attach yarn to edge of bottom band.

FINAL ROW Work same as for Collar.

Wrist Band (make 2)

SET UP Using MC and crochet hook, join yarn between two purl rows at seam on wrist edge of sleeve.

STARTER ROW 1 sc in same stitch as join, * skip 1, 1 sc in next stitch; repeat from * around, join with slip stitch to first sc, ch 3.

PATTERN ROW 1 dc in base of ch-3, * skip 1, 1 dc in next sc, skip 1, 3 dc in next sc (shell); repeat from * around, end with dc, join with slip stitch to first dc. Draw yarn through last stitch to fasten off, then break yarn.

Edge Trim

SET UP Using CC and smaller crochet hook, attach yarn to edge of Wrist Band.

FINAL ROW Work same as for Collar.

Finish

① Using a yarn needle and the yarn tails, sew six cherry bobbles to right front, six bobbles to left front, and two bobbles to each sleeve, clustered in pairs as shown in photo.

② Using perle cotton and blunt-tipped embroidery needle, sew stems for cherries in outline stitch.

outline stitch

③ Using the yarn tail and large-eye needle, sew buttons firmly to button band.

CHAPTER 3

Touch of Home

Granny-Square Afghan with Wide Knitted Border

Get ready to snuggle up in this colorful granny-square afghan. Making the basic granny square in a unique color palette updates the look. Adding the lacy knit border makes it unique. Stitch the border separately and sew it on as you knit it up.

Finished Measurements
50" × 59" (1.3 m × 1.5 m)

Yarn
Brown Sheep Cotton Fleece,
   80% cotton/20% wool,
   3.5 oz (100 g)/215 yds (197 m)
CA = 2 skeins #220 Provincial Rose
CB = 2 skeins #660 Blush
CC = 3 skeins #625 Terracotta Canyon
CD = 5 skeins #455 Willow Leaf

Tools
Knit US #7 (4.5 mm) straight needles, or
   size you need to obtain correct gauge
Crochet Size I/9 (5.5 mm) crochet hook, or
   size you need to obtain correct gauge

Gauge
Knit 1 pattern repeat = 2" × 2"
   (5 cm × 5 cm)
Crochet 1 square = 9" × 9"
   (22.5 cm × 22.5 cm)

Other Supplies
Large-eye yarn needle

Abbreviations
CA = contrasting color A
CB = contrasting color B
CC = contrasting color C
CD = contrasting color D
ch = chain (verb)
ch- = chained loop or chained space
dc = double crochet
K2tog = knit 2 together
sc = single crochet
yo = yarn over

Crocheting the Granny Afghan

Granny Square (make 30)

START UP Using CA and crochet hook, ch 4, join with slip stitch to form a ring.

ROUND 1 Ch 3 (counts as 1 dc), work 2 dc over ring, ch 2. * Work 3 dc over ring, ch 2; repeat from * two more times, join with slip stitch to third chain of ch-3. Draw yarn through last stitch to fasten off, then break yarn.

ROUND 2 Attach CB in any ch-2 space. Ch 3, 2 dc in same ch-2 space, ch 1, * (3 dc, ch 2, 3 dc) in next ch-2 space, ch 1; repeat from * two more times. 3 dc in beginning ch-2 space, ch 2, join with slip stitch to third chain of ch-3. Draw yarn through last stitch to fasten off, then break yarn.

ROUND 3 Attach CC in any ch-2 space. Ch 3, 2 dc in same ch-2 space, ch 1, * 3 dc in next ch-1 space, ch 1, (3 dc, ch 2, 3 dc) in next ch-2 space, ch 1; repeat from * two more times. 3 dc in next ch-1 space, ch 1, 3 dc in beginning ch-2 space, ch 2, join with slip stitch to third chain of ch-3. Draw yarn through last stitch to fasten off, then break yarn.

ROUND 4 Attach CD in any ch-2 space. Ch 3, 2 dc in same ch-2 space, ch 1, * (3 dc in next ch-1 space, ch 1) twice, (3 dc, ch 2, 3 dc) in next ch-2 space, ch 1; repeat from * two more times. (3 dc in next ch-1 space, ch 1) twice, 3 dc in beginning ch-2 space, ch 2, join with slip stitch to third chain of ch-3. Draw yarn through last stitch to fasten off, then break yarn.

ROUND 5 Attach CA in any ch-2 space. Ch 3, 2 dc in same ch-2 space, ch 1, * (3 dc in next ch-1 space, ch 1) three times, (3 dc, ch 2, 3 dc) in next ch-2 space, ch 1; repeat from * two more times. (3 dc in next ch-1 space, ch 1) three times, 3 dc in beginning ch-2 space, ch 2, join with slip stitch to third chain of ch-3. Draw yarn through last stitch to fasten off, then break yarn.

ROUND 6 Attach CB in any ch-2 space. Ch 3, 2 dc in same ch-2 space, ch 1, * (3 dc in next ch-1 space, ch 1) four times, (3 dc, ch 2, 3 dc) in next ch-2 space, ch 1; repeat from * two more times. (3 dc in next ch-1 space, ch 1) four times, 3 dc in beginning ch-2 space, ch 2, join with slip stitch to third chain of ch-3. Draw yarn through last stitch to fasten off, then break yarn.

ROUND 7 Attach CC in any ch-2 space. Ch 3, 2 dc in same ch-2 space, ch 1, * (3 dc in next ch-1 space, ch 1) five times, (3 dc, ch 2, 3 dc) in next ch-2 space, ch 1; repeat from * two more times. (3 dc in next ch-1 space, ch 1) five times, 3 dc in beginning ch-2 space, ch 2, join with slip stitch to third chain of ch-3. Draw yarn through last stitch to fasten off, then break yarn.

ROUND 8 Attach CD in any ch-2 space. Ch 3, 2 dc in same ch-2 space, ch 1, * (3 dc in next ch-1 space, ch 1) six times, (3 dc, ch 2, 3 dc) in next ch-2 space, ch 1; repeat from * two more times. (3 dc in next ch-1 space, ch 1) six times, 3 dc in beginning ch-2 space, ch 2, join with slip stitch to third chain of ch-3. Draw yarn through last stitch to fasten off, then break yarn.

Joining the Granny Squares

SET UP Arrange granny squares right-side up, in six rows of five squares each.

JOINING ADJACENT SQUARES Using CD, insert crochet hook from right side into corner ch-2 space of first square, pull up a loop, sc in same space, ch 1, insert hook from right side into corresponding ch-2 space of second square and work slip stitch, * ch 1, skip 1 stitch of first square, slip stitch from right side in next stitch, ch 1, skip 1 stitch of second square, slip stitch from right side in next stitch; repeat from * to end of seam. Break off yarn. Repeat to join five squares for each row. Make six rows.

Joining Rows

Repeat the joining technique to join the rows together.

Crocheting an Edge

Attach CD in any stitch, sc in same stitch, * (ch 1, skip 1 stitch, sc in next stitch); repeat from * to corner, (sc, ch 2, sc) in corner space **; repeat between * and ** three more times; repeat from * one more time, end ch 1, sc in joining chain. Draw yarn through last stitch to fasten off, then break yarn.

Pattern Stitch

Knit Border Pattern Stitch

ROWS 1, 3, 5, 7, 9, AND 11 Knit across row.

ROW 2 K3, K2tog, yo, K2tog, yo, K1, yo, K1.

ROW 4 K2, (K2tog, yo) twice, K3, yo, K1.

ROW 6 K1, (K2tog, yo) twice, K5, yo, K1.

ROW 8 K3, (yo, K2tog) twice, K1, K2tog, yo, K2tog.

ROW 10 K4, yo, K2tog, yo, K3tog, yo, K2tog.

ROW 12 K5, yo, K3tog, yo, K2tog.

Knitting the Border

① With CC and straight needles, cast on 9 stitches and work in Knit Border Pattern Stitch until piece measures about 52" (1.3 m), or until it is about 4" (10 cm) longer than one long edge of the afghan. Sew the border to the afghan edge, gathering it as you round the corner so that it lies flat. (See illustration below.)

② Continue knitting the Knit Border Pattern Stitch until the piece is about 4" (10 cm) longer than one short side of the afghan. Sew the border to the afghan edge, fitting it around the corner as before.

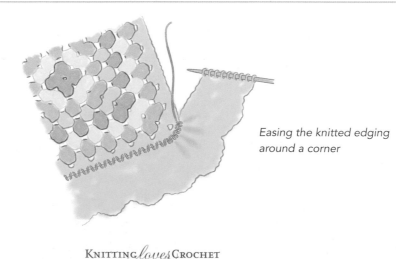

Easing the knitted edging around a corner

Finish

① Continue knitting the border and stitching it to the afghan edge as described opposite until you come to the beginning of the border. Cast off all stitches. Sew together the beginning to the end.

② Weave in any remaining loose ends.

Peek-a-Boo Pillows

Warm up any space with the vibrant colors of these fun and funky pillows. The fronts are crocheted squares made with large spaces so you can show off the colorful lining. Back it all up with a simple knit backing to provide stability. Worked in an easy-care cotton.

Finished Measurements
12" (30 cm) square

Yarn
Rowan Handknit Cotton, 100% cotton, 1.75 oz (50 g)/93 yds (85 m)
4 balls #316 Slippery

Tools
Knit US #7 (4.5 mm) straight needles, or size you need to obtain correct gauge
Crochet Size G/6 (4.25 mm) crochet hook, or size you need to obtain correct gauge

Gauge
Knit 18 sts and 24 rows 4" × 4" (10 cm × 10 cm) in Moss Stitch Pattern Stitch
Crochet 1 square = 6" × 6" (15 cm × 15 cm)

Other Supplies
Large-eye yarn needle
3/8 yd (34 cm) silk fabric, to complement yarn
12" (30 cm) square pillow insert

Abbreviations
ch = chain (verb)
ch- = chained loop or chained space
dc = double crochet
hdc = half double crochet
sc = single crochet
tr = treble crochet

Pattern Stitch

Moss Stitch Pattern Stitch

ROW 1 * K2, P2; repeat from * to end of row.

ROWS 2 AND 4 Knit the knit stitches and purl the purl stitches.

ROW 3 * P2, K2; repeat from * to end of row.

Crocheting the Motifs (make 4)

SET UP Using crochet hook, ch 6, join with slip stitch to form a ring.

ROUND 1 Ch 1, 16 sc into ring, slip stitch to first sc. You now have 16 sc.

ROUND 2 Ch 6 (counts as 1 dc and ch-3), skip 1 stitch, (1 dc into next stitch, ch 3, skip 1 stitch) seven times, slip stitch to third chain of ch-6.

ROUND 3 Ch 1, * (1 sc, 1 hdc, 5 dc, 1 hdc, 1 sc) into next ch-3 space [1 inner petal made]; repeat from * seven more times, slip stitch to first sc.

ROUND 4 Ch 1, * 1 sc between 2 sc, ch 6; repeat from * seven more times [eight arches made], slip stitch to first sc.

ROUND 5 Ch 1, * (1 sc, 1 hdc, 6 dc, 1 hdc, 1sc) into next ch-6 arch [1 outer petal made]; repeat from * seven more times, slip stitch to first sc. Draw yarn through last stitch to fasten off, then break yarn.

ROUND 6 Join yarn to first hdc of outer petal, ch 1, 1 sc into same place as ch-1, ch 6, skip 2 dc, 1 sc into next dc, * (ch 6, 1 sc into first hdc of next outer petal, ch 6, skip 2 dc, 1 sc into next dc); repeat from * seven more times, ch 3, 1 dc into first sc. Ch 3, turn (counts as 1 dc).

ROUND 7 3 dc in arch formed at close of Round 6, * ch 3, 1 sc into next arch, (ch 4, 1 sc into next arch) twice, ch 3, ** (4 dc, ch 3, 4 dc) into next arch; repeat from * two more times, and between * and ** one more time. End 4 dc into last chain arch, ch 3, slip stitch to top of ch-3. Draw yarn through last stitch to fasten off, then break yarn.

Knitting the Back

SET UP Using straight needles, cast on 54 stitches.

Work Rows 1–4 of Moss Stitch Pattern Stitch until piece measures 12" (30 cm) from beginning. Bind off all stitches in Pattern Stitch. Draw yarn through last stitch to fasten off, then break yarn.

① Arrange Crochet Motifs in two rows of two squares each. Using yarn needle, sew motifs together in pairs along edges. Sew the pairs together to complete Front.

② With wrong sides facing, place Front and Back together. Using yarn needle, sew pieces together on three sides. Turn piece right-side out.

③ Measure and cut two pieces of silk fabric, 13" × 13" (32.5 cm × 32.5 cm).

④ Place fabric pieces together with right sides facing and hand- or machine-stitch around three sides, taking a seam allowance of ½" (1.25 cm). Trim diagonally across corners. Turn piece right-side out.

⑤ Insert pillow form into silk cover and sew opening closed.

⑥ Insert pillow form into crocheted and knitted piece, then sew opening closed.

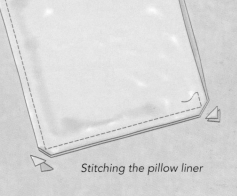

Stitching the pillow liner

Mix-and-Match Pillows

The perfect accent for any room, these throw pillows are fun and fashionable. Two different knit tops worked in a textured slip stitch make the perfect counterpoint for the Ultrasuede backs. The durable fabric backs offer a unique look and are easy to attach to the fronts with a simple crochet stitch. Just get out your hole punch and you're ready to go.

Finished Measurements
Large Pillow
   18" (45 cm) square
Small Pillow
   14" (35 cm) square

Yarn
Rowan Handknit Cotton,
   100% cotton, 1.75 oz
   (50 g)/93 yds (85 m)
Large Pillow
MC = 3 balls #316 Slippery
CA = 1 ball #239 Ice Water
CB = 1 ball #309 Celery
CC = 1 ball #219 Gooseberry
Small Pillow
MC = 3 balls #316 Slippery
CA = 1 ball #239 Ice Water

Tools
Knit (large pillow only)
   US #10½ (7 mm) straight
   needles, or size you need
   to obtain correct gauge
Knit (small pillow only)
   US #9 (5.5 mm) straight
   needles, or size you need
   to obtain correct gauge
Crochet (both pillows)
   Size F/5 (4 mm) crochet
   hook, or size you need to
   obtain correct gauge

Gauge
Knit (large)
   22 sts and 30 rows =
   4" × 4" (10 cm × 10 cm)
   in Slip Stitch Pattern Stitch
Knit (small)
   18 sts and 30 rows =
   4" × 4" (10 cm × 10 cm)
   in Slip Stitch Pattern Stitch
*Note: No gauge is required
for the crochet in this pattern.*

Other Supplies
Rotary cutter, cutting grid,
   and self-healing mat
½ yd (45 cm) Ultrasuede
   fabric (for two pillows)
Marking pen
Ruler
⅛" (.3 cm) hole punch
Pillow inserts
Large: 18" (45 cm) square
Small: 14" (35 cm) square
Large-eye yarn needle

Abbreviations
CA = contrasting color A
CB = contrasting color B
CC = contrasting color C
ch = chain (verb)
ch- = chained loop or
   chained space
hdc = half double crochet
MC = main color
sc = single crochet

Pattern Stitch

Slip Stitch Pattern Stitch for Large Pillow

Check your gauge occasionally as you work, as this pattern stitch has a tendency to get smaller.

ROW 1 * K1, move yarn to front, slip 1 purlwise, move yarn to back; repeat from * to end of row.

ROW 2 * P1, move yarn to front, slip 1 purlwise, move yarn to back; repeat from * to end of row.

Slip Stitch Pattern Stitch for Small Pillow

ROW 1 With MC, knit to end of row.

ROW 2 Knit to end of row.

ROW 3 Slip 1, then change to CA. * K2, slip 1 purlwise; repeat from * to end of row.

ROW 4 * Move yarn to front, slip 1 purlwise, K2; repeat from * to last stitch, slip 1.

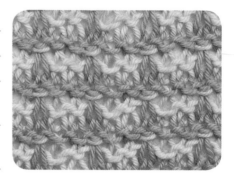

Knitting the Small Pillow Front

NOTE Measure your gauge occasionally as you work. This pattern stitch has a tendency to tighten up and get smaller as the piece develops.

SET UP Using MC and straight needles, cast on 64 stitches.

ROWS 1–4 Work Rows 1–4 of Slip Stitch Pattern Stitch for Small Pillow.

NEXT ROWS Repeat Rows 1–4 until piece measures 14" (35 cm) from cast-on edge. Bind off in Pattern Stitch. Draw yarn through last stitch to fasten off, then break yarn.

Knitting the Large Pillow Front

SET UP Using CA and straight needles, cast on 88 stitches.

ROWS 1–3 Work 3 rows of Slip Stitch Pattern Stitch. Change to CB.

ROWS 4–6 Work next 3 rows of Slip Stitch Pattern Stitch. Change to CC.

ROWS 7–9 Work next 3 rows of Slip Stitch Pattern Stitch. Change to CA.

NEXT ROWS Repeat these 9 rows, alternating Rows 1 and 2 throughout to create striped pattern until piece measures 18" (45 cm) from cast-on edge. Bind off in Pattern Stitch. Draw yarn through last stitch to fasten off, then break yarn.

Crocheting the Edging

Preparing the Fabric Back

① Using the rotary cutting tools and the Ultrasuede fabric, measure and cut a square — 14" (35 mm) — 18" (45 cm)

② Place fabric piece wrong-side up on flat surface. With a marking pen and ruler, mark a series of dots 3/8" (9 mm) apart and 1/4" (6 mm) in from edge all around.

③ Using a hole punch, punch a hole at each dot.

Edging

SET UP Use MC for the small pillow and CA for the large pillow.

ROUND 1 Using a crochet hook, insert hook into any hole through right side of fabric, pull up a loop, ch 3 (counts as 1 sc and ch-1), * (insert hook into next hole through right side, 1 sc, ch 1) to corner, 3 sc in corner; repeat from * three more times, continue as established to starting point, slip stitch into second chain, ch 2, turn.

ROUND 2 * 1 hdc in each stitch to corner, 3 hdc in middle sc at corner; repeat from * to starting point, slip stitch into second chain. Draw yarn through last stitch to fasten off, then break yarn.

Place Front and Back wrong sides together. Using CA and yarn needle, sew pieces together on three sides. Insert pillow form and sew remaining side closed.

Elegant Placemats and Napkin Rings

Breakfast in bed, romantic dinner for two — any way you serve it you might as well make it beautiful. This graceful placemat is knit in a simple slip stitch that allows it to lie flat. Artful crochet is worked around the entire piece to give it a romantic edge. Create a matching napkin ring using the same knit and crochet stitches. If you're so inclined you can whip up a whole table full to impress your guests.

Finished Measurements
Placemat 11" × 15" (27.5 cm × 37.5 cm)
Napkin Ring 6" (15 cm) diameter × 1¼" (3 cm) wide

Yarn
(makes 2 placemats and 2 napkin rings)
Aunt Lydia's Fashion Crochet Cotton, 100% cotton, 1.75 oz (50 g)/150 yds (137 m)
MC = 4 balls #625 Sage
CA = 1 ball #182 Lime
CB = 1 ball #175 Warm Blue

Tools
Knit US #10 (6 mm) straight needles, or size you need to obtain correct gauge
Crochet Size F/5 (4 mm) crochet hook, or size you need to obtain correct gauge

Gauge
Knit 20 sts and 30 rows = 4" × 4" (10 cm × 10 cm) in Slip Stitch Pattern Stitch using double yarn
Crochet 18 sts and 20 rows = 4" × 4" (10 cm × 10 cm) in sc

Other Supplies
Large-eye yarn needle

Abbreviations
CA = contrasting color A
CB = contrasting color B
ch = chain (verb)
ch- = chained loop or chained space
dc = double crochet
hdc = half double crochet
MC = main color
sc = single crochet
st(s) = stitch(es)
yo = yarn over

Pattern Stitch

Slip Stitch Pattern Stitch

ROW 1 * K1, move yarn to front, slip 1 purlwise, move yarn to back; repeat from * to end of row.

ROW 2 * P1, move yarn to back, slip 1 purlwise, move yarn to front; repeat from * to end of row.

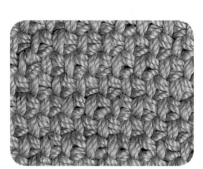

Bobble Pattern Stitch

Yo, draw up a loop, yo, draw through 2 loops on hook; repeat from * 3 more times; yo and draw through all 5 loops on hook, leaving a long tail for attaching.

Knitting the Napkin Ring

SET UP Using a double strand of MC and straight needles, cast on 30 stitches.

REPEAT ROWS 1 AND 2 of Slip Stitch Pattern Stitch until piece measures 1¼" (3 cm) from beginning. Bind off in pattern stitch. Draw tail through last stitch to fasten off, then break yarn. With right sides facing, sew together the short ends to form a ring.

Crocheting the Edging

NOTE Work Crochet Edging on both edges of napkin ring.

SET UP Using crochet hook, join a single strand of CA to edge of ring. With right side of ring facing you, * 1 sc in first 2 stitches, skip 1 stitch; repeat from * around ring. Join with slip stitch to first sc. You now have 21 sc. Ch 5, turn. (The ch-5 counts as 1 dc and ch-2 in Round 1.)

ROUND 1 * 1 dc in sc, ch 2, skip next sc; repeat from * around ring. End by joining last ch-1 to third chain of ch-5. Change to a single strand of CB. Do not turn.

ROUND 2 * 1 sc in each dc, 1 Bobble Pattern Stitch in each ch-2 space; repeat from * around ring. End with slip stitch to first sc. Change to a single strand of CA. Ch 2, turn.

ROUND 3 * 1 sc in sc, ch 4; repeat from * around ring. End with slip stitch to ch-2. Draw tail through last stitch to fasten off, then break yarn.

FINISHING Weave in all ends.

Knitting the Placemat

SET UP Using a double strand of MC and straight needles, cast on 56 stitches.

Repeat Rows 1 and 2 of Slip Stitch Pattern Stitch until piece measures 15" (37.5 cm) from beginning. Bind off in pattern stitch. Draw yarn through last stitch to fasten off, then break yarn.

Crocheting the Edging

then
Crochet

NOTE Although the smooth side of the knitting is usually considered the right side, you may prefer to place the textured side faceup.

SET UP Using crochet hook, join a single strand of CA 1 stitch beyond a corner of placemat. With right side of placemat faceup, work sc around as follows:

On long edges (row edge), work 1 sc in every other row.

On short edges (stitch edge), * (1 sc into 1 stitch) twice, insert hook into next stitch and pull up a loop as if to sc, insert hook into next stitch, pull up loop, and complete sc through all loops on hook (1 sc made in 2 stitches); repeat from * across edge.

At each corner, work 3 sc.

When you reach starting point, join with a slip stitch to first sc. Ch 5, turn (ch-5 counts as 1 dc and ch-2 in Round 1).

ROUND 1 Skip 1 stitch, * (work 1 dc in next stitch, ch 1, skip 1 stitch) to corner, (dc, ch 2) in each of the 3 corner stitches; repeat from * around placemat. Join last ch-1 to third chain of ch-5. Change to a single strand of CB. Do not turn.

ROUND 2 Work * 1 sc in each dc, 1 Bobble Pattern Stitch in each ch-1 space; repeat from * around placemat. End with slip stitch to first sc. Change to a single strand of CA. Ch 2, turn.

ROUND 3 Work * 1 hdc into sc of Round 1, ch 4; repeat from * around placemat. End with slip stitch to top of ch-2, ch 2, turn.

ROUND 4 Work (1 sc, 1 hdc, 3 dc, 1 hdc, 1 sc) in each ch-4 space, end with slip stitch into first sc. Draw tail through last stitch to fasten off, then break yarn.

FINISH Weave in ends.

Christmas Berries Stocking

Traveling vines wind their way around this basic stocking to make it a holiday treat. The winter white knit stocking provides the perfect backdrop for the sparkly crocheted flowers and berries. Santa will surely look forward to filling this stocking.

Finished Measurements
Length 6" × 19½" (15 cm × 48.8 cm)
Width at heel 7½" (18.8 cm)

Yarn
Patons Classic Merino Wool, 100% wool,
  3.5 oz (100 g)/223 yds (205 m)
MC = 1 ball #202 Aran
Patons Brilliant, 69% acrylic/31% polyester,
  1.75 oz (50 g)/166 yds (152 m)
CC = 1 ball #4942 Radiant Red

Tools
Knit One set US #7 (4.5 mm) double-point
  needles, or size you need to obtain
  correct gauge
Crochet Size F/5 (4 mm) crochet hook, or
  size you need to obtain correct gauge

Gauge
Knit 22 sts and 28 rows = 4" × 4"
  (10 cm × 10 cm) in Stockinette Stitch
Crochet 20 sc = 4" (10 cm)

Other Supplies
3 stitch markers
Small stitch holder
Large-eye yarn needle
2 skeins DMC perle cotton, medium green

Abbreviations
CC = contrasting color
ch = chain (verb)
ch- = chained loop or chained space
dc = double crochet
hdc = half double crochet
K2tog = knit 2 together
MC = main color
P2tog = purl 2 together
sc = single crochet
ssk = slip, slip, knit these 2 stitches
  together
St st = stockinette stitch
tr = treble crochet
yo = yarn over

Knitting the Stocking

SET UP Using MC and double-point needles, cast on 60 stitches. Distribute evenly on three needles. Join, taking care not to twist stitches. Place a stitch marker at beginning of round.

ROUND 1 * K2, P2; repeat from * to marker.

ROUNDS 2–12 Repeat Round 1. Ribbing now measures 2" (5 cm).

NEXT ROUNDS Knit all stitches. Work even in stockinette stitch (knitting every round) until piece measures 12" (30 cm). End at marker.

Heel Flap

SET UP Knit 14 stitches, place next 32 stitches on a stitch holder, place last 14 stitches at beginning of needle with first 14 stitches. In this section, you will be working back and forth on only two double-point needles. *You now have 28 sts on one double-point needle.*

ROW 1 (WRONG SIDE) Slip 1, P27.

ROW 2 * Slip 1, K1; repeat from * to end of row.

ROWS 3–20 Repeat Rows 1 and 2.

Turning the Heel

ROW 1 Slip 1, P15, P2tog, P1, turn. You are leaving 9 sts unworked.

ROW 2 Slip 1, K5, ssk, K1, turn. You are leaving 9 sts unworked.

ROW 3 Slip 1, purl until 1 stitch remains before gap formed by last turning, P2tog, P1, turn.

ROW 4 Slip 1, knit until 1 stitch remains before gap formed by last turning, ssk, K1, turn.

ROWS 5–12 Repeat Rows 3 and 4 four more times, until turning gaps are closed, ending with a knit row; do not turn. *You now have 16 sts.*

Instep

SET UP Using crochet hook and double-point needles, pick up and knit 11 stitches from side of heel, knit 32 stitches from stitch holder, pick up and knit 11 stitches from other side of heel, knit 16 stitches from needle. Divide stitches evenly among three double-point needles. From here, you will again be knitting in the round. *You now have 70 sts.*

STARTER ROUND Knit to stitch marker.

ROUND 1 K16, K2tog, place stitch marker for instep shaping, K34, place stitch marker for instep shaping, ssk, K16. *You now have 68 sts.*

ROUNDS 2, 4, 6, AND 8 Knit to end of round.

ROUNDS 3, 5, 7, AND 9 Knit until 2 stitches remain before first stitch marker, K2tog, knit to next stitch marker, ssk, knit to end of round. At end of Round 9, *you now have 60 sts.*

ROUND 10 Knit, removing 2 instep stitch markers.

NEXT ROUNDS Work even until foot measures 6" (15 cm) from heel.

Shaping the Toe

ROUND 1 K13, K2tog, place stitch marker for toe shaping, ssk, K26, K2tog, place stitch marker for toe shaping, ssk, K13.

ROUND 2 Knit until 2 stitches remain before first stitch marker, K2tog, ssk, knit until 2 stitches remain before second stitch marker, K2tog, ssk, knit to end of round. *You now have 56 sts.*

ROUNDS 3–12 Repeat Round 2 ten times. *You now have 16 sts.*

Remove remaining stitch marker. Bind off. Using MC and yarn needle, sew toe closed.

Crocheting the Embellishments

EDGING AROUND TOP Using CC and crochet hook, attach yarn to top edge of stocking. Work 1 sc in each stitch, join with slip stitch to first sc. Draw yarn through last stitch to fasten off, then break yarn.

Heel Stripes

Using CC and crochet hook, insert hook from right side into stitch above first slip stitch on heel flap, pull through loop, skip 1 stitch, insert hook into next stitch, pull loop through loop on hook (1 ch stitch made). Continue in this manner to work chain stitch "stripe" along slip stitch valley, pull yarn tail through to wrong side and secure. Break off yarn. Make 13 stripes, one in each slip stitch valley of the heel flap.

Flowers (make 6)

SET UP Using CC and crochet hook, ch 4, join with slip stitch to form ring.

ROUND 1 * Work 1 sc into ring, ch 3; repeat from * four more times.

ROUND 2 Work (1 hdc, 1 dc, 1 tr, 1 dc, 1 hdc) into each ch-3 space, join with slip stitch to first hdc. Draw yarn through last stitch to fasten off, then break yarn.

Berries (make 16)

Using CC and crochet hook, ch 3, * yo, insert hook into third chain from hook and draw up a loop, yo, draw through 2 loops on hook; repeat from * two more times. Yo and pull yarn through all 4 loops on hook. Pull yarn through last loop to fasten off, then, leaving a long tail for attaching berry to stocking, break yarn.

Finish

① Using perle cotton and crochet hook, work chain stitch as for heel stripes across surface of stocking to create meandering vines as shown in the drawing below.

chain stitch

② Using CC and yarn needle, sew flowers and berries firmly to stocking along vine, as shown in photo at right and drawing below.

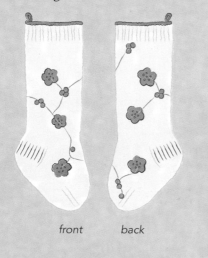

front   *back*

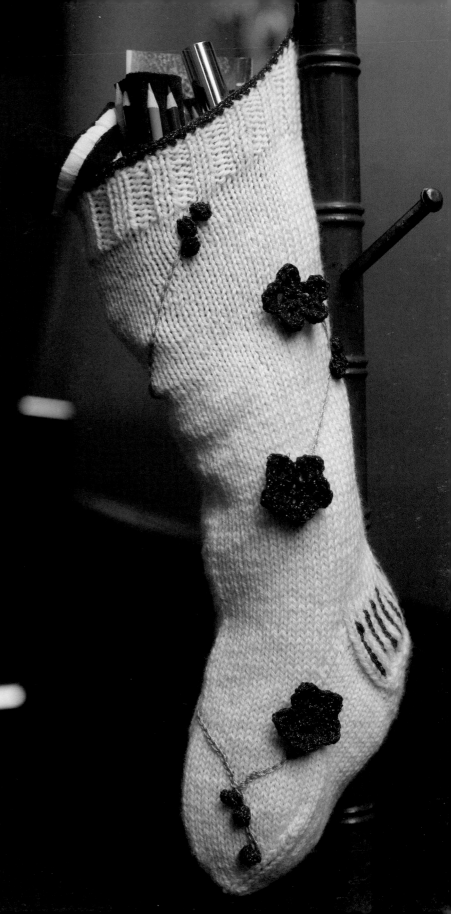

Glossary

AS ESTABLISHED. Continue working the same stitch pattern or shaping as in previous rows/rounds. *See also Stitch pattern.*

ASTERISK (*). *See also Repeat.*

BIND OFF. Also known as Cast off. To remove knit stitches from needle in a manner that keeps them from unraveling. A common bind-off is as follows:

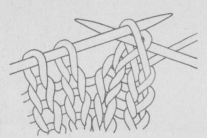

bind off

① Knit 2 stitches, insert the left-hand needle into the front loop of the stitch knit first, lift the loop over the stitch knit second, and remove the first stitch from the right-hand needle.

② Knit another stitch, and lift the first stitch over the second in the same way.

③ Continue to knit 1 stitch and lift old stitches over new until you have bound off the required number of stitches.

NOTE When one stitch remains, cut the yarn, leaving a 6" (15 cm) tail, then pass the tail through the last stitch and pull to tighten.

CAST ON. To put stitches onto the needle to begin a knitted piece. The long-tail cast-on is one common method, and it is worked as follows:

① Leaving a long tail (allow approximately ½–1"/1.25–2.5 cm per cast-on stitch, depending on needle size), make a slip knot and place loop on needle. With the needle in your right hand, hold the tail and the working end of the yarn in your left hand, as shown.

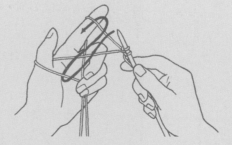

② Insert the needle through the front loop of the tail on your thumb from front to back. Bring the needle tip over the top and behind the working yarn on your finger. Use the needle to draw the working yarn through the tail loop on your thumb.

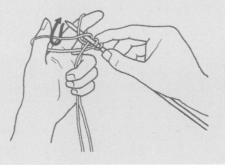

③ Release the tail loop on your thumb, place your thumb underneath the tail, and pull both yarns to tighten while holding both firmly against your palm.

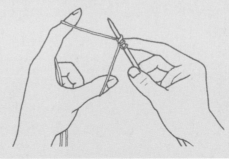

CHAIN (CH). Make a slip knot and place loop on hook. Wrap the yarn over the hook from back to front (yo) and pull a loop through the loop on the hook (1 chain made). Repeat until you have the right number of chains. Each chain stitch forms a V on the front of the chain. To count stitches, include each V, but do not count the slip knot or the chain on the hook. The back of the chain looks like a series of bumps.

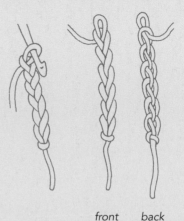

front   *back*

DECREASE (DEC). To reduce the number of stitches being worked, 1 or 2 stitches at a time. For *knitting*, *see also* Knit 2 stitches together, Pass the slipped stitch over, and Slip, slip, knit. Decreasing is different from binding off (*see* Bind off). For *crochet*, most decreases are accomplished using the slip stitch (*see* Slip stitch).

DOUBLE CROCHET (DC). May be worked into a chain or into the tops of crochet or knit stitches in an existing piece. To practice, make a chain of 11 stitches.

① Bring yarn over hook from back to front. Insert hook into fourth chain from hook.

② Bring yarn over hook again, pull it through to front, move it to shank. You now have three loops on hook.

③ Bring yarn over hook again and draw it through the first two loops on hook.

④ You now have two loops on hook.

⑤ Bring yarn over again from back to front and pull it through the two remaining loops on hook.

⑥ You have now completed a double crochet.

⑦ Repeat steps 1–6 across row, working in the next chain for each stitch.

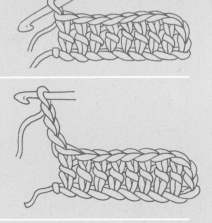

⑧ Before you turn to work a second row, chain 3 stitches. This turning chain is the start of the second row, and you need to make one at the end of each row of double crochet.

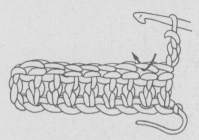

⑨ Turn work counterclockwise. Yarn over from back to front, insert hook into top two loops of second chain from hook, then repeat steps 2–6. Continue in this way, inserting hook into top two loops of each stitch to end of row.

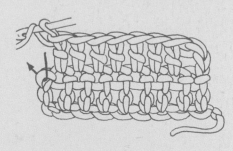

⑩ Insert hook into top of last chain and complete your last double crochet. Make a chain-3 turning chain as before. Turn, and crochet to end of next row, then work last double crochet in top stitch of turning chain from previous row (at arrow).

FASTEN OFF. To end a row or round in such a way that the work will not unravel. Work until 1 loop/stitch remains on hook/needle. Cut yarn, leaving a 6" (15 cm) tail. Pass the tail through the last stitch and pull to tighten. (See also Bind off; Round; Row; Tail)

FOUNDATION CHAIN. The chain worked at the beginning of a crochet piece.

GARTER STITCH. When using straight needles, knit all stitches on every row, whether wrong- or right-side rows.

HALF DOUBLE CROCHET (HDC). May be worked into a chain or into the tops of crochet or knit stitches in an existing piece. To practice, chain 11.

① Bring yarn over hook from back to front. Insert hook into third chain from hook.

② Yarn over and draw yarn through chain to front, then move it to shank of hook. You now have three loops on hook.

③ Yarn over again from back to front and pull it through all three loops on hook.

④ You have now completed a half double crochet.

⑤ Repeat these steps in each chain across row.

⑥ Before you turn to work a second row, chain 2 stitches. This turning chain is the start of the second row, and you need to make one at the end of each row of half double crochet. Yarn over and insert hook into second stitch in row.

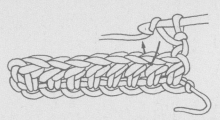

⑦ Repeat steps for half double crochet across row, working into both top loops of each stitch until you get to chain 2 (turning chain) of previous row.

Insert hook into top chain of turning chain and complete your last half double crochet. Chain 2 and turn as before.

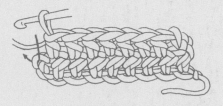

INCREASE (INC). To add stitches, one or two at a time. For knitting, *see also* Knit 1 front and back and Make 1. For crochet, increase by working 2 or more stitches into the same stitch in the previous row, or by working into edge stitches that would otherwise be skipped.

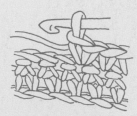

increase in crochet

IN PATTERN. To continue working in the stitch pattern while working shaping instructions or binding off. (*See also* As established; Bind off.)

JOIN NEW YARN. (*See also* Weave in ends.) In knitting, fold the new strand 6" (15 cm) from the end (to leave a tail to be woven in later), place the fold on the right-hand needle, and work the next stitch. After working several stitches, pull gently on the tail of the new strand to tighten the first few stitches to the same tension as the rest of the piece. In crochet, new yarn is commonly joined with a slip stitch, or work as follows:

Work until 2 loops remain on hook, drop the old yarn (or cut, leaving a 6" [15 cm] tail), and work the last 2 loops with the new yarn.

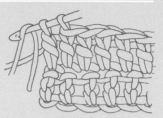

joining new yarn

KNIT 1 FRONT AND BACK (INCREASE 1). Knit the next stitch, then, without dropping the stitch from the left-hand needle, knit the same stitch through the back loop and drop stitch from left-hand needle. This kind of increase, also called a bar increase, leaves a small bar or bump at the base of the second stitch. In this book, it is the recommended method for "increase 1."

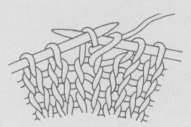

increase in knitting

KNIT 2 STITCHES TOGETHER (K2TOG). Insert the right-hand needle into the second and first stitches on the left-hand needle from left to right (as if to knit) at the same time. Knit them together as if they were 1 stitch.

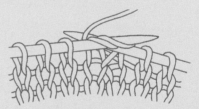

knit 2 together

KNITWISE. Positioning the right-hand needle in the normal manner for knitting, with the tip of the needle going into the front of the stitch on the left-hand needle from left to right.

MAKE 1 (M1). An increase method done as follows:

For a left-slanting stitch, insert the tip of the left-hand needle from front to back into the strand of yarn between the stitch just worked and the next stitch.

Lift the strand to the left-hand needle, then knit it through the back loop, twisting it to close the hole.

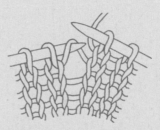

make 1 left

For a right-slanting stitch, pick up the strand from back to front.

Knit it through the front loop, twisting the strand to prevent a hole.

make 1 right

markers

MARKER. Used to indicate pattern sections or to mark the beginning of a round when working circularly. In knitting, slip either ring markers or split-ring markers right onto the needle. In crochet, use only split-ring markers, and move them from the marked stitch row by row.

PASS THE SLIPPED STITCH OVER (PSSO). Used in knitting when decreasing. Slip 1 stitch, knit the next stitch, then use the left-hand needle to lift the slipped stitch over the knit stitch and drop it off the needle.

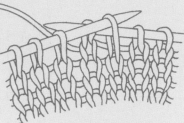
pass slipped stitch over

PICK UP STITCHES. To begin a new section of the piece by picking up along a knit or crocheted edge, using a knitting needle or a crochet hook. For information and illustrations of different pick-up techniques, see pages 20–21.

PICOT. A small loop or other decorative pattern stitch, usually used on edges of pieces.

PLACE ON HOLDER. To remove a stitch or section of stitches that will not be worked for several rows or that will be used later during finishing and hold them on either a stitch holder or a piece of scrap yarn until needed.

PURL 2 STITCHES TOGETHER (P2TOG). Insert the right-hand needle into both of the next 2 stitches on the left-hand needle from right to left (as if to purl), then purl them together as if they were 1 stitch. (See also Decrease.)

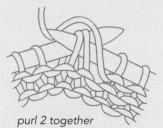
purl 2 together

PURLWISE. Positioning the right-hand needle in the normal manner for purling, with the tip of the needle going into the front of the stitch on the left-hand needle from right to left.

REPEAT (REP). To work the indicated number of stitches either after an asterisk * or enclosed in brackets [ ] or parentheses ( ), the number of times specified in the instructions. Note: In this book, after brackets or parentheses the total number of repeats is indicated; after an asterisk, the number indicates how often you should repeat in addition to working the sequence the first time (for example, "two more times").

RIGHT SIDE. The side of the fabric meant to be the "public" side. In a garment, it is the side worn facing out, away from the body.

RING. In crochet, to begin a ring, chain the indicated number of times, then insert your hook into the first chain. Yarn over, then draw the yarn through both the chain and the loop on the hook with no further yarn overs. (See also Slip stitch.)

crocheting a ring

ROUND. A round begins and ends at the same point. (See also Marker.)

In knitting, a round is complete when all stitches have been worked once when working circularly (with circular or double-point needles). It's helpful to use a marker to indicate the beginning and end of rounds.

In crochet, a round is complete when all stitches have been worked without turning. You may indicate the end of the round with a marker and join the round with a slip stitch, or you may work rounds in a continuous spiral.

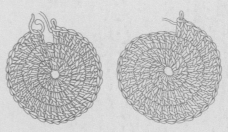

ROW. One row is complete when you have worked straight from the first stitch to the last stitch.

SINGLE CROCHET (SC). May be worked into a chain or into the tops of crochet or knit stitches in an existing piece. To practice, make a chain of 6 stitches.

① Insert hook through second chain from hook.

② Bring yarn over hook from back to front.

③ Pull yarn to front and move it to shank of hook. There are now two loops on hook.

④ Bring yarn over hook again from back to front and pull it through both loops on hook.

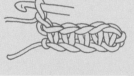

⑤ Now you have one loop on hook, and you have completed 1 single crochet.

⑥ Insert hook into next chain and repeat process until you have reached the end of the chain. Do not crochet into slip knot itself. You should see five stiches in the completed row. Don't forget to count as you work.

⑦ Before you turn to work a second row of single crochet, chain 1. This is called the turning chain. Now, turn piece counterclockwise so back is facing you.

⑧ Work first single crochet into last single crochet of previous row. This time, insert hook under both top loops of first single crochet and repeat steps 2–5.

⑨ Continue in this way across row and in subsequent rows until piece is desired length. You'll find it helps to count stitches as you work, so that you don't gain or lose any.

⑩ To end piece, cut yarn, leaving about a 6" (15 cm) tail, then pull yarn completely through last loop to fasten off.

SLIP MARKER. In knitting, move the marker from the left-hand to the right-hand needle when you come to it and continue working. In crochet, move the marker from the marked stitch up to the next row/round. (*See also Marker.*)

SLIP, SLIP, KNIT (SSK). Slip 2 stitches one at a time as if to knit and move them on the right-hand needle. Return them to the left-hand needle in turned position, then knit them together through the back loops. **TIP** To avoid stretching the leading stitch, work with just the tip of the needles.

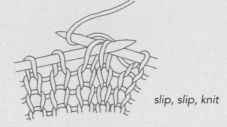

slip, slip, knit

SLIP STITCH. In knitting, moving a stitch from the left-hand needle to the right without working it. This can be done knitwise or purlwise. (*See also Knitwise; Purlwise.*)

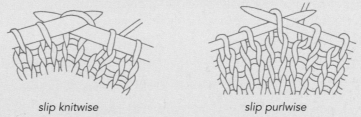

slip knitwise   *slip purlwise*

In crochet, a way of either joining or moving across a stitch without adding height. Insert hook into top of stitch and draw yarn through both top loop of stitch and loop on hook without any yarn overs.

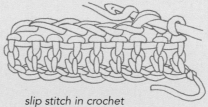

slip stitch in crochet

SPACE. In crochet, the eyelet (hole) created when a series of chains were worked in the preceding row or round. Instructions may indicate that you crochet into a space rather than into a stitch.

STITCH PATTERN. A number of stitches worked over one or more rows or rounds in a specific sequence to produce the texture of the fabric unique to the piece being knitted or crocheted. The instructions indicate how many stitches are in the stitch pattern and how many ties to repeat the sequence. (*See also* Repeat.)

STOCKINETTE STITCH. When using straight needles, stockinette stitch is worked by knitting all stitches on right-side rows and purling all stitches on wrong-side rows. When using circular needles, all stitches are knit on every round.

stockinette stitch, right side　　　　*stockinette stitch, wrong side*

TAIL. A strand of yarn, 6" (15 cm) or more long, left when beginning and ending use of that yarn. In knitting, both casting on and binding off leaves a tail. In crochet, tails remain from the foundation chain and when fastening off. In both knitting and crochet, you also have tails when you join a new ball of yarn or change colors within a row or round. You can neatly weave in the tail during finishing or use it to sew seams or reinforce color joins. (*See also* Weave in ends.)

THROUGH THE BACK LOOP. Insert the right-hand needle into the part of the next stitch that lies behind the left-hand needle and work from that position. Working stitches through the back loops results in twisted stitches, a decorative feature of some stitch patterns.

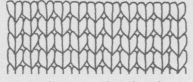

Knitting through the back loop

TRIPLE CROCHET (TR). Also known as treble crochet. May be worked into a chain or into the tops of crochet or knit stitches in an existing piece. Practice by chaining 11.

① Bring yarn over hook twice from back to front.

② Insert hook into fifth chain from hook and yarn over.

③ Pull yarn through chain to front and move it to shank of hook. You now have four loops on hook.

④ Bring yarn over again from back to front and pull it through first two loops on hook. You now have three loops on hook.

⑤ Yarn over again. Pull yarn through next two loops on hook.

⑥ You now have two loops on hook.

⑦ Yarn over one more time and pull yarn through last two loops on hook.

⑧ Repeat these steps across row.

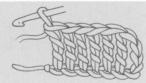

⑨ Before you turn to work a second row, chain 4 stitches. This turning chain is the start of the second row, and you need to make one at the end of each row of triple crochet.

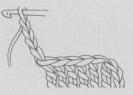

⑩ Yarn over twice and insert hook under both top loops of second stitch from hook. Repeat steps 3–7.

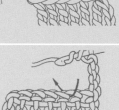

⑪ Continue in this way, working into both top loops of each stitch across row, until you get to chain 4 (turning chain) of previous row. Insert hook into top chain of turning chain and complete your last triple crochet.

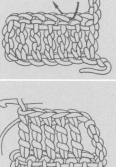

⑫ Chain 4 and turn as before.

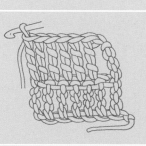

TURN. Work across all stitches to the end of the row, or to the point specified in the instructions, then rotate the piece so that the opposite side of the work is facing. When working straight, turn at the end of every row in both knitting and crochet, unless the instructions state otherwise. (See also Row.)

TURNING CHAIN. One or more chains worked at the beginning of a row or round to raise the next row or round up to the appropriate level. The pattern stitch you are using determines the number of chains required for the turning chain. The turning chain that begins the next row is sometimes counted as the first stitch(es) of the next row/round. This will be stated in the parentheses in the directions the first time it occurs, but may not be stated for subsequent rows or rounds.

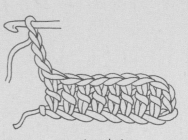

turning chain

WASTE YARN. Small bits of yarn left over from previous projects. Use for stitch markers or stitch holders.

WEAVE IN ENDS. This is done to secure tails left when beginning and ending a piece or when joining new yarn. (*See also* Join new yarn; Tail)

In knitting, you can weave the tail in by taking it over and under the working yarn as you knit, or, when the project is finished, you can use a large-eye yarn needle to weave in the tail on the wrong side along the same row of stitches.

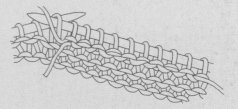

weaving in the tail as you knit

In crochet, thread the tail on a large-eye yarn needle, and neatly run the end in and out of a few stitches on the wrong side of the piece.

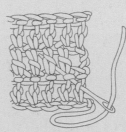

weaving in the tail on a crochet piece

WRONG SIDE. The side of the fabric meant to be the "private" side. In a garment, the wrong side is worn against the body; in a stitch pattern, the less attractive side may be designated as the wrong side.

YARN OVER (YO).

In knitting, bring the yarn to the front between the needles (the purl position, if it is not already there), lift it up and over the needle to the knit position, then place it in the correct position to work the next stitch.

yarn over in knitting

In crochet, wrap the yarn around the hook from back to front so that the strand is caught in the head of the hook, then draw the yarn through as specified in the instructions. (May also be stated as yarn over hook or yarn around hook.)

yarn over in crochet

Needles and Hooks

Knitting Needle Sizes	
METRIC	U.S.
2.25 mm	1
2.75 mm	2
3.25 mm	3
3.5 mm	4
3.75 mm	5
4 mm	6
4.5 mm	7
5 mm	8
5.5 mm	9
6 mm	10
6.5 mm	10½
8 mm	11
9 mm	13
10 mm	15
12.75 mm	17

Crochet Hook Sizes	
METRIC	US
2.25 mm	2 steel, B/1
2.5–2.75 mm	C/2
3.0–3.25 mm	D/3
3.5 mm	E/4
3.75–4.0 mm	F/5
4.0–4.25 mm	G/6
4.5 mm	G/6, 7
5 mm	H/8
5.5 mm	I/9
6.0 mm	J/10
6.5–7.0 mm	K/10.5
8 mm	L/11
9 mm	M,N/13
10 mm	N,P/15
15 mm	P,Q

Acknowledgments

It has been said many times, but it's true . . . these books don't get done alone. There are many people involved in the process who make my work easier and who make me look much better.

First of all, I couldn't do any of this without the flying fingers and dedication of Joyce Nordstrom. She is the backbone of my little operation and along with her group of helpers, Judy Timmer and Jane Lind, she makes my work so much easier. Many thanks to the wonderful craftswomen who helped me "get things done yesterday," Audrey Sakai, Betty Feinstein, and Mary Woods.

My creativity is enhanced tenfold by the brilliant people who have made this book look so beautiful: Mary Velgos, Art Director and book designer; Donna Demari, photographer; Robin Tesoro, photo stylist; and Christine Erikson, illustrator. An especially big, huge, I-can't-do-it-without-you to Gwen Steege, my editor extraordinaire, who is always supportive and a very special friend.

Finally, I want to share my gratitude for all the people who stand by me and make it possible for me to do what I do. My husband, Tom, who still makes me smile; my grandson, Johnny, who loves me no matter what; Heather and John, for allowing me to spoil Johnny and providing me with another "soon-to-be" grandchild; my son, John, who has overcome so much; my Mom, Jean, and sister, Rajeana, who are my biggest supporters; and to all my close friends who put up with my "no shows" because of work. You guys make me a better person.

Storey Publishing would also like to express appreciation to Donna Demari, photographer; Douglas Feeney, photographer's assistant; Robin Tesoro, photo styling; Rosemary Redlin & Gigi Vega, hair and makeup styling; and models Lida Egorova, Nicole Fiscella, and Alena Semanenka.

Shot on location at the Porches Inn and MASS MoCA in North Adams, Massachusetts. Special thanks to Derek Kresiak, Katrina Skiffington, Dorothy Mason, Jodi Chappell, and the rest of the staff at Porches.

Index

Page number in *italics* indicate photographs and drawings. Page numbers in **bold** indicate tables.